A legerman's dream

GORDON WOOD

LEGERING

Tackle & Techniques

STANLEY PAUL

London · Sydney · Auckland · Johannesburg

Stanley Paul and Co. Ltd
An imprint of Century Hutchinson

Brookmount House, 62–65 Chandos Place,
Covent Garden, London WC2N 4NW

Century Hutchinson Australia (Pty) Ltd
88–91 Albion Street, Surry Hills, NSW 2010

Century Hutchinson New Zealand Limited
191 Archers Road, PO Box 40–086, Glenfield, Auckland 10

Century Hutchinson South Africa (Pty) Ltd
PO Box 337, Bergvlei 2012, South Africa

First published 1989

Set in 10pt Baskerville Linotron by
Tek Art Ltd, Croydon, Surrey

Printed and bound in Great Britain by
Butler & Tanner, Frome, Somerset

British Library Cataloguing in Publication Data
Wood, Gordon
    Legering : tackle and techniques.
    1. Angling
    I. Title
    799.1'21.

ISBN 0 09 174041 X

For my father, who encouraged me to wet a line at a very early age. For my brother Paul who stayed with the sport and for my brother Bernard who didn't. But most of all for my dear late mother, who suffered in silence over the years while making endless pots of tea for visiting anglers. Sadly, Mum, the kettle has now gone off the boil.

Gordon Wood

January 1989

ACKNOWLEDGEMENTS

Fred J. Taylor, for the foreword; Gerry Hughes, for the loan of his extensive library; David Bird, for details concerned with lead and swan deaths; Victor Wood, for the illustration captioned 'A Legerman's Dream'; and Matthew Wright for assisting with the photography.

The Tackle Trade: R. I. Brightwell, of Abu Garcia; Kevin Nash; John Roberts; Barry Welham, of Leeda; W. R. Thurston, of Bitech Viper Ltd; Nigel Tovey, of Varitech Tools; Chris Ogborne, of Kamasan; G. Griffin, of Auto Fish Feeders; E. R. Sarbutts, of Mustad; John Loftus, of Shimano; J. R. Wright, of Enak; and Peter Drennan.

Contents

Foreword
by Fred J. Taylor

Back in the 1950s when legering was referred to as 'splodging with semi-eel tackle', the whole of the match-angling world fell about laughing when Dick Walker suggested that one day the National Championship (the All-England, as it was then) would be won by an angler using leger tackle. It was unthinkable at the time, and I had my own doubts about it. I had, however, seen how effective the rolling leger could be when a very young angler (none other than Peter Stone, as it turned out) gave me a fishing lesson. I was pegged next to him in a friendly Thames competition and I saw another side to angling.

It seemed, in those days, that most anglers started off by selecting their float for the day and then shotted it to suit the needs dictated by the prevailing water conditions. Walker suggested that, instead of deciding what float to use, we should perhaps ask ourselves if we needed one at all. If we decided we could do without a float, we should then ask whether or not we actually needed any lead! We should build up from there.

Legering had been practised for many years before that and those horrendous (by today's standards) coffin leads and bored bullets had already proved successful for the better-quality fish of the Thames. I believe, however, that anglers began to *think* about legering around that time.

The National *was* won on the leger eventually (by Ken Smith of Norwich) and this success, added to the development of the earlier swing-tip (invented by an angler named Clayton who had previously slated legering) began the trend. Quiver and spring-tips followed. Float styles and float patterns continued to be developed, and today the choice is almost frightening. Legering, however, became something of a cult among specimen hunters and some of the traditional float skills were wasted on them. That was unfortunate.

It has been a very interesting progression and it has all been set down here in very readable form by Gordon Wood, author of thought-provoking articles in the angling press over a period of many years.

This is not yet another 'how to do it' or 'how I dunnit' book but a thoughtful work on the history, development and practice of legering – none of which suggests that there is nothing technical to learn from it. There is. I have read it and I ought to know!

Introduction

Angling as we know it with rod and line goes way back to the time of the ancient Egyptians and beyond. This much we have learned from sculptures found in ancient tombs and also from illustrations in old Egyptian scripts depicting anglers whose angling method was without doubt the leger. Well, that's what my eyes tell me! In 1908, J.W. Martin (the 'Trent Otter') wrote '. . . It may very nearly be taken for granted that the capture of fish as a staple article of food was among Man's very earliest pursuits . . .' He also suggested that spears and nets of earlier times were used to catch fish and were undoubtedly the precursors of fishing with an angle. 'Angling,' he added, 'became an art before it became a sport . . .', or putting it more prosaically, the art of fishing progressed to satisfy the need to fill bellies whereas the sporting aspect developed once they were full.

Casting with a well-balanced multiplying outfit reminds me that the feeling I enjoy is an art form. I derived enormous satisfaction from it because the cast has been controlled every inch of the way by thought and application, attributes which are required to a lesser degree by exponents of the fixed-spool, as I'm sure those familiar with both kinds of reel would agree – as would J.W. Martin himself, had he access to the well-precisioned multipliers we take so much for granted today.

Martin also put forward Tubal-Cain as the first teacher in metals to find a place in the history books, and as such also the first true angler, since he is credited with making the very first metal fishing hook. And legering must surely have been the simplest way to present a bait, for it takes no imagination at all to visualise even a troglodyte casting into a fish-filled pool with a length of some primitive form of line attached to the middle of a splinter of wood sharpened to a point at both ends so as to act as a gorge when the bait was taken and the line pulled. Even the classic fishing match of all time, that between Antony and Cleopatra, was a contest in leger fishing! I think the prominent Victorian angler-author Francis Francis must have been in agreement with what has been said because he wrote: 'Bottom fishing is the most primitive style: we all more or less began with bottom fishing.' and assuming that he might have used the term 'legering' rather than bottom fishing when making the statement in his book *Angling*, published in 1877, we might also assume this his use of the word 'primitive' was not intended as a reproach to the method itself but to infer that our approach to fishing was simplified to the point where the very roots of angling lie.

A legered bait as the Oxford Dictionary tells us is a fishing bait which is made to remain in one place – to lie on the bottom, and has in the past been deemed a lazy man's method, requiring nothing more strenuous than the mere casting of the bait, after which comes the waiting for something to happen. Disciples of legering will decry this description as nonsense, while acknowledging deep down perhaps that, yes indeed, we have met that kind of angler, but on fewer occasions than can be counted on the fingers of one hand – it is so in my case at least.

The well-known but unattributable observation about fishing as being 'a fool at one end of the line and a worm at the other' was most likely made with a float-fisher in mind, lost and oblivious to everything around him in a dream world of his own, since it surely doesn't reflect the legerman's attitude to his sport. He is generally more observant; more calculating; and when the pressure is really on, more inclined in the end to come up with something that's a bit revolutionary with which to outwit the fish.

For legering in one form or another is without a doubt the most intriguingly complex angling technique of all. It is also now the most popular. Indeed, even though it did take an excessively long time for anglers to get the message and see the light, even the match-fishing fraternity now forsake their floats when the need arises to fill their nets by using the leger instead. So why

**Even match anglers turn to the leger when the need arises,
a fact registered at weigh-ins**

then is the method such a tremendous hit? The answer to that
question can be summed up in two words: *Big Fish*! For there
can be no denying that the legered bait is far more likely to
ensure success. But, of course, the issue goes far deeper than
that. We have to consider tackle control, in itself no simple task

on a windswept water with anything but a well-weighted line; and let's not forget the casting accuracy required in getting a bait to the fish, particularly when fishing at long range. Legering also affords the angler a more interesting proposition than other methods, even though all methods must inevitably have their day, fish being the contrary creatures that they are. As we all know, when in the mood, fish will go out of their way to do what we least expect of them – but that's angling in a nutshell, of course. And if one legering rig fails to get the better of them, it's a certainty that another will, be it the most complicated of carp rigs or a bait offered on nothing but the hook and line. All rigs and tackles have their moments of glory, and each in one form or another has seen the light of day before. That's one of the peculiarities of angling, and especially of legering – there is little that can be hailed as being truly new, absolutely original, or quite without equal or precedence somewhere down the line. That in turn gives us a deep well of knowledge from which to draw when all else fails. Our interest in legering, then, need

Legering accounts for better fish. This cased chub (present NASA record) weighed a colossal 8 lb 4 ozs. It was taken in 1913 by a Mr G.F. Smith, and is believed to have accepted a legered sliver of liver!

Mark Lucas, winner of the 1988 Sealink Classic Fishing Festival, achieved his success on the leger

never falter. How can it, when there is so much on offer?

Finally, for the purpose of this book, the expression 'lead' is used throughout. This is of course intended to refer to safe lead, but to emphasise as much by continuously referring to it would be boring, and so I ask for your sympathy and understanding in this respect.

The Initiation

I was probably about six or seven when I first threw out a line with a sinker attached, having finished with a float after a fashion long before then. It is more than likely that the bait on the leger would have been worm; it always was when my father and I were after eels at night. We didn't want anything else to gulp it down and nothing else ever did as those long glorious days of summer faded into sultry evenings and nights spent out in the open under the stars, young as I was at the time. They passed all too quickly, though, while waiting for the not-unkind-to-the-nose smell of methylated spirit to signify that dear old Dad was lighting the primus for a brew-up in the middle of the night – a smell which even today, takes me back in time to those golden moments of childhood quicker than anything else.

For the chub my father and grandfather pulled out dispassionately year after year it was always huge cubes of cheese. Not a single one comes to mind which was tempted on worm. I've no idea why, unless the gimp wire attached to the hooks used for worms put off the chub. I have long since come to rate a lob or two on the hook as one of the finest chub baits ever. And true to form we always fished at the very same spot on the lower Thames at Laleham, with never a diversion to another swim, never mind a different reach of the river, save for the very odd occasion when we would fish in front of the rowing-boat house at Molesey instead. There it was again worms for the eels, and those same whacking great pieces of cheese for the many fine roach that fed freely throughout the hours of darkness. Like the chub at Laleham they too would spurn altogether our more meaty offerings of worms.

The London Blitz was in full swing by then and, what with his duties as an air-raid warden and the like, my father found it impossible to get to the river as often as he would have liked. Yet still we managed to wet a line together often enough. In retrospect I suppose I was probably better off on the riverbank over the weekends away from home and the bombings.

The only lights permissible at the time had to be well shielded from prying German eyes, so the bicycle lamps we used for fishing had a metal shield in front of the glass to throw the light downwards. Dough bobbins and bells on pegs were the bite detectors used, while the rods were right out of this world, consisting of a billiard cue for the butt and an officer's swagger stick for the top section, and believe me, a fish had to be pretty beefy to put up a show on that kind of gear – and yet somehow they did. Perhaps they really were bigger then!

For reels we used the old wooden Starback or Nottingham type of centre-pin. What else, when the fixed-spool, spinning or threadline reel as it was then known was still waiting to be afforded by the vast majority of anglers? Few had as yet clapped eyes on this most innovative of creations, let alone actually used it. In fact, those same few were probably the only ones to know that such a reel existed at all, so out of reach was it for most people. And, indeed, not even monofilament line was available then. The nearest we got to it was thick square-shaped stuff we called catgut, on which we ran our leads. For reel line it was invariably 12 lb Cuttyhunk, which had to be laid out carefully on the road running parallel to the river and then cast by holding the line with one hand and the rod with the other, releasing the line held in check at just the right moment to let the weight (always a coffin lead) take the bait out.

And believe it or not, in this fashion we managed to put those baits way out, almost to the other side of the river more often than not. It sure was an eerie sight, though, to see others bent double as they laid their lines out upon the ground prior to casting – like giant black crabs is how I always thought of them when silhouetted against the moonlight. Crouched low to the ground and clawing at the invisible line as they swayed with a sideways gait, they must have frightened the life out of many a poor old lady enjoying an evening stroll with her pooch. But that was the way of fishing then, and a favourite tale of my father's concerns the morning my grandfather spread his line meticulously out on the road and was just in the throes of casting when along came a milk cart pulled by a very sleepy horse – and away went Grandad's line on its hoofs. You don't get yarns like that to tell these days!

Sadly, Grandad didn't live long enough to see the arrival of the fixed-spool reel and the like, but it's doubtful if he'd have entertained one in any case, after a lifetime of painstakingly laying out his line on the ground. But suddenly there they were on the distant horizon. I was still a schoolboy at the time and it was in the classroom that I got the first inkling that such a thing existed. I saw a photograph of one in a magazine, in which a cigarette was used to demonstrate what little weight was needed to steal line from the spool – which still wasn't fixed incidentally, the true fixed-spool reel emerging later, as far as I can determine. But what need had I then of knowing about such trifling matters? Here at last was the means to enable me to spin for pike, or so I thought when just a few years later I purchased my very own spinning reel.

An Allcocks Stanley it was, on which the line was recovered by way of a claw-like hook; and 35 shillings (or £1.75) is what I paid for it second-hand. That happened to be the better part of a week's pay just then, but after staring at the thing in the shop window every night for a week before finding the courage to squander such a princely sum on it, how proud I was when leaving the shop with it tucked safely in my pocket. And what a great big wonderful new world it was going to open up for me. Alas, the sorry conclusion to this little tale is that my splendid reel turned out to be anything but, what with the way it twisted my line and all. And then, after all that, now that I could do it after a fashion, I discovered that spinning didn't really appeal to me; so it was post-haste back to the leger, from which I have never since departed.

1 Legering Rods

Legering rods are, like the sport itself, difficult to pigeon-hole in terms of when they first made an appearance. But if we return again to the ancient Egyptians we shall find evidence in the murals they left behind of rods being used to catch fish, and that was around 2000 BC! The rods were not only tapered but in two pieces, which rather surprises me since if they were that advanced it's a wonder those Egyptians of old didn't see the advantages to be had from a wand of a single length (assuming the material was to be had in such lengths). A one-piece rod bends into a more natural curve for casting as well as playing the fish – although, admittedly it's doubtful if attention to such fine detail would have mattered when seeking fish just for the pot.

Papyrus reeds more than likely became the source material for the first rods (as suggested in that mighty tome *Falkus and Buller's Freshwater Fishing*, by Fred Buller and Hugh Falkus), because they grew alongside the River Nile; and reeds of one kind or another continued to find themselves wearing a coat of light varnish, bindings and rings right up until the likes of glass fibre came on to the scene to replace them (although with built-cane trying hard to become fashionable again this material is still meeting something of a need, however limited at the present time).

Other more solid materials have also left their mark. Green-heart, for instance, was a very firm favourite during both the nineteenth and twentieth centuries, although it was heavy and unwieldy if not fashioned with due care, and the tips were apt to be very unforgiving, as I discovered to my cost on more than one occasion. Yet for all that, many sang the praises of green-heart rods, so perhaps I never came to appreciate their true value. Lancewood and hickory were also used for the making of fishing rods, although the latter was more prized in the form of walking sticks. And let's not forget the willow wand so idolized by Izaak Walton! Willow was as popular in his day as carbon is in ours. It may be extremely hard to imagine the 'father of angling' and his ilk trying actually to leger with any worthwhile weight on the end of that flimsy excuse for a fishing rod, until one glances at some of the rods in use today. However slack in appearance they do the job nevertheless. But that does not necessarily apply to the willow, which makes any achievement of old with it all the more creditable in my book.

But somewhere along the line (and it was actually written about as early as the 1600s!) the bright idea was conceived of making a rod from different kinds of wood: with cane or lancewood for the tip and the middle section, if it was a three-piece effort, and with something less worthy like hickory for the butt. It then came to pass that somebody, somewhere began to split cane in order to make fishing rods, but I don't know who or where. Was it in England? The USA? Both are equal contenders, since each was producing split-cane rods well over a hundred years ago. But as usual there's a question mark, for similar poles, rather than rods, were being aired long before then – way back in 350 BC in fact.

It was most likely during the 1930s when split-cane began to make its presence felt more widely. With a tonkin cane for the middle joint and Spanish reed for the butt joint, split-cane was more often used for the tip of the rod, until F.W.K. Wallis arrived in the south and brought with him his trent style of fishing. Split-cane then rapidly became the middle as well as the top joint, and tonkin cane became the butt, at which point World War II intervened to stop all further progress in the development of the fishing rod until long after peace had been restored in 1945.

With no materials available for unnecessary pastimes like fishing, the situation called for a great deal of DIY (indeed, the trend towards do-it-yourself so much in evidence today could owe its initial roots to those just demobilized from the Forces and trying to gear up again for fishing or some other pursuit.)

I can remember quite distinctly rummaging through the debris of bombed-out buildings for a suitable piece of flexible steel that my father might be able to turn into a landing-net rim. The rods that had survived the bombings now kept the curtains in place, with the exception of one that my father had brought home when on leave from Brussels. That, to my dying shame, was swapped for the timber needed for a rabbit's hutch! Dad was not best pleased, although why I don't know. It was just a float rod after all!

The best most anglers could do to replace war-torn legering rods was to haunt the markets and search the barrows for billiard cues to use as fishing rod butts, and golf clubs or officers' swagger sticks for the tips. When trimmed down with a knife and finally a sheet of sandpaper these at least in some measure resembled the rods which had served well enough in the past, however lacking in flexibility. There was no lacking of flexibility in initiative, however, and eventually many legermen discovered tank aerials. When made into leger rods they were superb, and so cheap it was possible to have identical pairs, although the temptation to keep buying tiny tins of enamel paint to change the colour of them was always present. But at last we were out of the mire, and forging onward to even greater things!

Aluminium rods – usually telescopic – put in a brief appearance next, and should have shown us then where the true materials for rod-making lie; but it was also about this time that split-cane became more readily available. With Dick Walker's MK IV carp rod and then the lighter version, the Avon, leading the field for the newly found interest in specimen hunting, there couldn't possibly be any other material to use. Indeed, there's a nice little tale that goes with the rod on which Dick actually caught his carp, Clarissa, after which the former was kept in a glass case. Along came Chris Yates, holder of the present carp record, with a request to give the old and highly historical rod an airing. Right away it accounted for a beautiful twenty-pounder, and was then put back in its case (with even more reverence, I shouldn't wonder). Twice I've seen this rod on display, originally at the National Angling show in London in 1965 and then at the Carp Society's Conference in Luton,

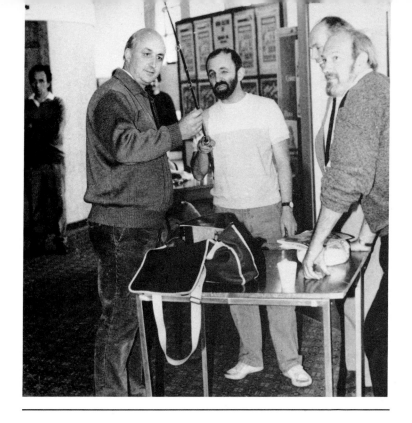

A rod with a tale to tell. Dick Walker's MK IV, on which he smashed the carp record, is felt for 'vibes' by Walker fans

Bedfordshire in 1988, when I not only had the opportunity to handle but also to photograph this most charismatic of all rods.

Yet notwithstanding what Dick Walker did with it, split-cane had its faults, one being the set it tended to develop in no time at all if not nursed like a baby when in use. Considering the punishment from big fish it was supposed to endure, and the exorbitant asking price, I reckon we were entitled to expect

Times have changed and here a carbon rather than a cane rod is put away at the end of the day

more from it. In fact, while hesitating to say as much, since another rod-builder was much patronized at the time, I must nevertheless make it known that the only decent MK IV carp rod I ever had was made by Ogden Smith's. Went through hell, that rod did, on Norfolk pike especially; and yet, however unfashionable, it never let me down unlike others I tried.

Nevertheless it was sad in a way to see split-cane being superseded, not so much by solid glass-fibre rods, which were far too heavy and unforgiving for my liking, but rather the hollow glass-fibre ones that had a great deal going for them and didn't need a lot of caring for into the bargain. But there is still a small army of anglers who will consider nothing but dear old split-cane to take their fish, and if the quality of the cane is there then who can blame them for that? Never did a rod look more appealing – or businesslike – than a beautifully made split-cane job.

With them to a very large extent went full cork handles, to be replaced by the more durable – if somewhat disagreeable – duplon and hyperlon grip, which just don't have the feel or appearance of cork. It's interesting to note, also, that whenever an advertisement appears for a rod with a full cork handle, that point is always mentioned, which is not the case when other materials are used to dress the butt. So who knows, perhaps we'll eventually see a more positive return of the former. Agate-lined rings also vanished, and along came stainless steel, with Fuji battling its way to the fore with rod-runner design.

But to move on further we gradually left even glass-fibre lagging behind in favour of yet another wonderful creation, carbon-fibre, which is often used for rods in composite form. And that's the final word, most would say – but is it? I wonder. Boron is coming up fast on the inside lane, to pose the question of what might come next. Futuristic steps will perhaps be taken with rod design in mind rather than the materials from which it is made. Tri-cast, for instance, have recently released their revolutionary Senator Ext range of match and quiver rods, the length of which can be altered while actually fishing. Exactly where we go from there is anyone's guess!

2   Legering Reels

Since the dawning of Aquarius, so it seems, we've been blessed with fishing reels – used merely to contain the line at the very beginning, with no function whatsoever to bring into play in the duel between fish and man. First mentioned in English angling literature in 1651 (Thomas Barker's *The Art of Angling*), reels for fishing have in fact been known to exist long before that, and since Chinese paintings going back to the late twelfth century actually depict fishermen with makeshift reels on their equally makeshift rods, it has been assumed (and quite rightly, I think) that the fishing reel originated in China*.

Crude they were to say the least, but very effective for their day – so much so that in China, reels similar in almost every respect to those of a bygone age are still being produced, marketed and used widely at the present time. These are commonly known as spoke reels, and in appearance could be likened to a bicycle wheel in miniature, with hub and spokes. The absence of handles serves merely to accentuate the illusion. There is no drum as such and the line is contained around the rim of the reel in the protruding V-like shapes extending from each spoke: a design said to have been filched from the system that powered spinning wheels of old.

Line retrieval is achieved smoothly and rapidly by rotating the reel with a finger between the spokes, and it can be cast out again directly from the reel (although I wouldn't be keen to try it). The reel itself is affixed to the rod by a bolt passing right through it and kept in place by a tightened nut. It is also blessed with a drag of sorts, or an anti-reverse feature if you like – which just goes to show that in spite of popular belief the Japanese aren't the only orientals producing fishing gear!

*See *Falkus and Buller's Freshwater Fishing*, Stanley Paul, 1988

The first English reel (winch was the term used to describe them when I was a boy) was in all probability a winder instead, on which the line was wound as it was held in one hand while in the other was the rod. We can also safely accept that at one time loose line would have been wound around the rod top as a matter of course, and that shortly thereafter, a ring or two began to appear on rods even at that early stage.

The first reel to gain any credence would more than likely have looked something like an enlarged cotton reel, with a handle to crank on the line. This when looked at in perspective would have presented the most logical means of containing the line, and is a theory subscribed to by most who have dared to look that far back into angling history, I should think, because it lends itself so obviously to the need, particularly when one remembers that the cotton reel was already there to borrow the idea from. To suggest otherwise would, I feel, be stretching credibility to breaking point and beyond because angling, in this country at least, has always subsisted on the obvious and the uncomplicated (difficult as is the functioning of some rigs to unravel these days!).

Most of these 'ancient' reels were originally fixed to the rod by a pin going right through it, and later by a bracket that was clamped over the rod and by one means or another fastened to it. Often these brackets were lined with leather to give them a firmer grip on the rod, and were in continuous use until sliding reel fittings appeared towards the end of the nineteenth century. By then, though, multiplier reels had been around for a hundred years or more; and what puzzles me about published illustrations of those early multiplier reels is that the seating shown would have called for something a bit more substantial than the means mentioned above for securing the reel to the rod, which suggests that they were probably bound on, and tightly by all accounts, because multipliers have always been notorious for coming adrift from the rod if not suitably stabled, and that's a situation that hasn't changed in the least over the years.

What most brass reels had in common were very tiny and quite inadequate spindles on which the line was wound. They

Some fine reels from the past (*Ray Cannon Collection*)

were also around in quite surprising numbers during and even after World War II, and I personally had a couple in my bag when a boy. And there they stayed, condemned for evermore to a role of complete inactivity, and all because of that small ineffectual spindle which served no purpose other than to bury the line to an irretrievable degree.

But by then, of course, threadline reels were beginning to emerge in greater numbers, while most of us still had to make do with that old faithful the Nottingham type reel. This was designed in the middle of the 1800s, in the first instance for casting and controlling float tackle in the fast flow of the River Trent – although later models, blessed as they were with superior balance, were quite capable of casting leger leads and even spinners straight from the reel when in the hands of an expert. And what delightfully simple creations they were to be sure! With the drum running freely on a centre-pin, there really wasn't much that could go wrong with these fine pieces of

Ancient centre-pins. Note the fine quality and craftsmanship

ingenuity, which were originally made from wood. The better ones were known as Starbacks, due to the brass star-shaped bracing on the back, and were to lead the way some thirty years later to more renowned versions of the centre-pin reel, notably the celebrated Allcock-Aerial, which is skeletal in appearance and prized by so many today as the finest and undisputed champion of all centre-pin reels!

The fixed-spool reel

Contrary to widespread belief, the spinning, threadline or fixed-spool real is not an invention of the twentieth century. Yet with the emphasis placed on it today one could be excused for thinking otherwise, for rarely has an item of fishing gear been so readily accepted. Even in fly fishing I've known weighted wet flies to be cast from a fixed spool, and have used one myself often enough to present tiny natural baits to trout on a fly rod that was especially adapted with an elongated butt to take the reel.

The truth of the matter is, however, that the first reel capable of casting in the manner of a fixed-spool reel saw the light of day as long ago as 1878, when G.R. Holding came up with the idea of rotating a wooden Nottingham type of reel so that the line would spill from it like cotton from a bobbin with the least prompting. Malloch's metal reel came next (1884) and was said to be a vast improvement on Holding's, to the point where it is now a treasured collector's item.

But of course, that was only the beginning, and yet in a sense the end of reels that needed to be rotated in order to cast the line freely – or was it? Popular even today in Australia is the Alvey reel, which rotates in much the same manner for casting as did the two reels mentioned above. They were great clumsy wooden abominations when I used them last, but the spools are now fashioned from fibre-glass and as much as I abhorred them so the Aussies adored them, which might suggest that they knew something I didn't.

Also on to the market in the late forties and early fifties came that amazing little gadget known as the Adaptacast. This resembled a reel seat on one side which slid into the reel fittings of the rod, while on the other side were fittings to take the reel which the Adaptacast permitted to be rotated for casting. They cost five shillings (25p) at the time, but weren't a great commercial success as I recall, probably because most of the reels that would have been used in conjunction with it in those days had a drum that was too deep and thick at the rim to allow the passage of line to flow freely.

Before then, though, had come Alfred Illingworth's reels (1905), which in appearance at least were like a fixed-spool, and which were at one time commonly referred to as 'egg-beaters' due to their whisk-like action. Next in the chronological turn of events came the ever-popular Allcock-Stanley: a weird, meat-grinder of a reel that felt like one in use and was often referred to as a fixed-spool when in fact it was no such thing. It was the line-retrieve hook which was fixed, except when it worked piston-like in a vain attempt to lay the line evenly on the spool, which actually revolved. This, as mentioned elsewhere, was my first so-called spinning reel and owning it wasn't a pleasant experience, as fondly as I may think about it today!

Marketed in 1926 (or possibly around 1933, reports vary, depending on the source), the Allcock-Stanley was endowed with a price-tag equivalent to £1.13p, and appeared to take the same ridiculous amount of time to filter through to the man in the street as most spinning reels of this nature – or at least to the people I mixed with at the time, so what a bunch of down-and-outs we must have been! The Allcock company, nevertheless, claimed that during the first four years following its introduction 10,000 of these reels were sold (which was obviously a figure worth mentioning in those days) and never a one to me that wasn't second-hand!

But to advance to the time when threadline reels began to get through to the anxiously waiting hordes. In principle, at least, the clutch was intended to minimalize the risk of being busted by a fish when using the thread-like line recommended by the manufacturers at the time (hence the term threadline). Indeed, in practice, the angler's sole contribution to all this, so those same manufacturers would have had us believe, was simply to wind the reel and hope for the best – whether or not the fish was taking line at the appropriate moment – the idea being, of course, that the clutch would yield line irrespective of what the angler did!

Perhaps it was just as well, then, that those early promises were never fulfilled, otherwise we would all have ended up on the banks like zombies, winding wildly to bring in the fish; a picture that inspires me not in the least! There was, however, yet another reason put forward for the birth of the threadline, and I dare say a more honourable one which, in a nutshell, was unique in that it permitted line to be retrieved as soon as the lure hit the water to lessen the chances of it becoming snagged. There we have one of the original blurbs behind the production of these reels, and just where promotional fiction took over from hard facts is nigh on impossible to define now. But what does that matter? The reel had arrived in our midst, and for that we should remain eternally grateful.

Since Alfred Illingworth first gave us a taste of the good things to come (although in reality another inventor by the name

A fine collection of fixed-spool reels

of John Ray is credited with the first prototype of this kind of reel, a good thirteen years before Illingworth got round to it!), we have seen many other reels, all vying for a more prominent place on the market.

Among the better threadline or fixed-spool reels were Hardy's Altex, as one would expect (with a full bail pick-up, would you believe, even in 1932!), and the original Mitchell (with a half-bail claw pick-up when first produced in 1946 and also with push-button quick-change spool efficiency as perfected by the Romans 2,000 years earlier to secure their front doors). This reel was graced with the first optional anti-reverse facility too, so must have been something very special for its day.

The Ambidex was another top-quality reel, with an action as smooth as silk, while at the fence were left the likes of the Omnia (despite its space-age looks) and the Intrepid, which was cheap and serviceable up to a point; plus a few others that didn't even get past the starting post, in this humble scribe's opinion. Of them all, the Mitchell lived on to become the most popular fixed-spool reel of all time (yes, we can use the term fixed spool in all sincerity now!).

Exactly what the sales figures of Mitchells would show now I've no idea, but a few years back 30 million of these top-notch reels had been produced, distributed and sold, of which a little more than half had been the popular 300 model. Mitchells can also boast of having more casting records to their credit than all the other makes of reel put together, and that's saying something! One hundred and forty different modifications over the years have since enhanced the appeal of Mitchells even further, and no matter what alterations were made, inter-changeability in respect of handles and spools continued to exist.

Mitchells were not, however, the first to produce skirted reels. That accolade must go to the relatively unknown firm of Smith and Wall who brought out skirted reels way back in 1935. The Platil Line Co. gave us one in the late 1940s and Mitchells finally got into the act by the mid 1950s, to make their reels even more appealing in every respect. Some significance must also be given to the fact that whenever an angler brags of using a reel that is twenty years or more of age, it will inevitably turn out to be a Mitchell! My own 300s are even older, but with just a little care and attention at the start of each season I know they'll carry me through to the end of it without any serious mishap.

But be that as it may, there are now on the horizon to challenge cult reels like the Mitchell 300, contenders from Abu Garcia, with their line of Cardinal reels; Shakespeare with their successful line-up; and last but by no means least Shimano with theirs, including the Baitrunner series of reels, which is gaining ground at an amazing rate. These may give Mitchells a run for their money, but with the head-start the latter has over the newcomer, it'll require something extra special to take the lead with reels that will still be around and functioning as well as today's Mitchell 300s will be in a couple of decades from now, and I have it on good authority that Shimano's Baitrunners are just that. But only time will tell. . . .

Multipliers

Ever since I first learned to use one I've been fascinated by multipliers. Each cast with them is a lesson in itself; a challenge, which once met gives the user more satisfaction than a cast with a fixed-spool reel could ever aspire to. And it's all down to personal pride, of course. I've used multipliers successfully for more than twenty years, and first had an abortive attempt with one almost as many years before that. Yet still I get that delightful feeling of having achieved something rather special after each and every cast, which suggests to me at least that there's something very special about the reels.

You can become more attached to a multiplier than to any other kind of reel – apart, perhaps, from a particularly interesting centre-pin from the past, which conjures up that same old magic when handled. I shall never understand how even light spinners were worked on them, and I have a deep-seated admiration as well as a lasting respect for the old-timers who could rise to that kind of craftsmanship with a mere flick of the wrist. (Makes whatever we achieve with a fixed-spool look ludicrous by comparison, don't you think?) Not even multipliers (occasionally known as drum reels, overhead reels or geared reels) can claim to demand the skill those ancient centre-pins called for.

However, I still get extra pleasure from fishing with a multiplier, and find it sad that it is something that still remains in the realms of mystery for most anglers. If only they'd let their hair down and give a multiplier a whirl, they would soon discover that it's a myth they've been unnecessarily overawed by all these years.

Multipliers today are a dream to use! They're complex in design, but then so is the word processor I'm tapping away at now; but I wasn't going to let it get the better of me. It didn't, and neither will the multiplier get the better of you, unless you cower from it. So be firm; show the reel who's the boss by belting out a bait on it without a moment's hesitation. Sure, there will be birds' nests; that's all part of the learning process. But you'll be surprised at how seldom this happens, even during the initial stages of learning. I also promise you that once you've mastered the intricacies of these so-called 'infernal machines' you'll never look back!

I'm only sorry that when I first tried one it turned out to be a cheap and tinny imitation of what a good reel should be. I was just a teenager at the time, and therefore impatient: keen to forge ahead and leave behind all that didn't warrant my further attention. Left there for ever more then, or so I thought, was the possibility of my ever again attempting to cast with a multiplier. For I had failed miserably, most heart-breakingly, and had bitterly vowed never to touch one again. And neither did I, for a score of years or more, until there came the day when my brother Paul disclosed an interest in multipliers for fishing in Australian surf. Just as I had done a long time previously, however, he turned to a cheaper version of the reel and failed with it just as completely, at which point a friend came to the rescue with an offer to try his Ambassadeur 7000, the outcome of which was instant success!

Fuelled by the amazing distances Paul was able to attain in no time flat with his own newly acquired 7000, as compared with my own with a hugely overweight salt-water fixed-spool reel, I begged him to show me how it was done. And if there's a lesson to be learnt from this little tale, it is to leave cheaper versions of the multiplier alone. Go for the best you can possibly afford because, unlike fixed-spool reels of which even the cheapest and nastiest will serve its purpose after some sort of fashion, its counterpart in the multiplier division will serve no purpose at all other than to have you pulling your hair out by the roots in terrifying frustration. Believe me, I know.

But here again we have an item of fishing gear that goes way, way back – to the 1770s would you believe! And that's only when it was first mentioned in print, which might suggest that this particular type of reel existed for some time before then; and it didn't look so vastly different from today's models, either.

Credited originally as an American invention, by watchmaker George Snyder of Pennsylvania in 1810 (although as shown above, multipliers were in existence long before then), it is now accepted by those considered to be authorities on the subject

Close-up of the latest Abu Garcia multiplier reel

that the true origin of the multiplier lies with British inventors. But it was developed in practical terms by the Americans, who continued to use it to advantage while in this country the very idea of using a multiplier was left to gather dust. This shouldn't be so surprising when we learn that those early multipliers were actually placed under the rod instead of above it as today, making the casting of them an even more daunting proposition than most believe modern multipliers to represent. In fact the latter are no more difficult to cast than a fixed-spool reel, once mastered, and much can be achieved in a single practice session out in the garden.

The American company of Pflueger achieved world-wide fame when it produced in the 1930s the Supreme multiplier reel, which embraced most of the features found in such reels today, including an anti-backlash device, synchronized line-guard and a level-wind facility, which gave it the status of being

35

unique for its time. But then, several decades later, Abu of Sweden took up the gauntlet to challenge this domination by American multipliers by offering us the still unequalled, as far as I can see, range of Ambassadeur reels. Abu cast a huge net, and with one mighty sweep enmeshed in it contenders for sea, game and freshwater fishing with their Ambassadeur reels, which were soon extended even more to include the entire spectrum of angling (with the exception of fly fishing, of course).

Each reel bore the name of Ambassadeur and the different models were designated by a number, the most popular of these being the Ambassadeur 7000. The Abu Garcia family of multipliers continues to grow, and has a completely new design now, as can be seen in the 1989 range of freshwater reels, such as the Ambassadeur XLT Syncrodrag Reel. The syncrodrag is a new system which reduces the likelihood of a break by allowing the angler quickly to reduce his pre-set breaking power. This is engineered by a backward turn of the handle, after which a forward turn reverts the break to its original setting.

Other worthwhile multipliers are Leeda Mitchells, which I know are good because I've used them for years, (but I would like to see a lighter model on the market); Pen reels, which represent good value for money but are again, sadly, mainly a salt-water reel; and the Daiwa Millionaire reels. There are, of course, others which I cannot personally vouch for, but assume that in this day and age, providing you're not contemplating something which is obviously little better than a toy, the choice is very much down to individual taste.

But where on the freshwater fishing scene do multipliers

Author's multipliers used for coarse fishing. From top to bottom: an Ambassadeur 6500, which is a bit heavy overall for freshwater fishing; an Ambassadeur 5000, which is ideal for piking and eeling; and the latest Ambassadeur XLT model, which is designed specifically for pike, carp and other big fish

---

come into their own? Well, I've always thought they have a large role to play, particularly when it comes to piking, for multipliers are built for the job of subduing big fish, not to mention the casting of big deadbaits. The free-running spool, which can be regulated to avoid an over-run by a single turn of a knurled nut, is also ideally suited to pike fishing, as is the more direct contact these reels give the angler with a furiously fighting predatory fish. But don't just take my word for it; beg, buy, steal or borrow one to put you in a position to confirm as much for yourself.

By no means, however, are multipliers restricted to pike fishing. The Ambassadeur XLT model mentioned above has been specifically designed with carp in mind as well, and those behind its promotion are quite convinced that this reel will cause anglers to think anew when it comes to multipliers. They're probably right because it seems to have combined within its new-look outer casing a couple of facilities that have been missing on even the best multipliers for far too long. The need to cast overhead, for instance, has always been a drawback when fishing an overgrown swim, but the 'flipping' aid found only on some Ambassadeur reels (such as the XLT) is a boon to underarm or side casting in that it allows the immediate engagement of the spool.

More important in my opinion, though, is the number of multipliers now coming on to the market that have allowed for the angler who prefers to operate his reel with the left hand. This includes the majority of us who are naturally right-handed, and the failure to meet such a need previously has, I fear, retarded quite considerably and for an extremely long time the growth of this type of reel on the coarse-fishing scene. But now, at last, those concerned with such details have finally seen the light, with the result that in the future I'm sure we'll see more multipliers being put to the test, and while I can never see them replacing fixed-spool reels for the smaller species, I feel certain that the big fish specialist in particular is in for a very nice surprise.

3   Legering Leads

When looking at leger leads the first conclusion I come to is that the most useful and versatile of all sinkers is the humble and often neglected split-shot. These are still considered by some to have no function other than to weight a float, whereas in practice nothing could be further from the truth. It's the various sizes they come in which make split-shot such a useful commodity to the legerman, giving him the ability to be extremely exact in the amount of lead required to counteract varied conditions in respect to casting distance and combating the flow.

Split-shots are also easily attached to the line and removed again in a matter of seconds when the need arises, whether pinched directly on to the hook-link or on to a separate piece of

Figure 1   Split shot

line, stopped by either another split-shot or one of the more popular stops, such as a bead or plastic stop. And if ever I'm in doubt as to the amount of lead I should use, I invariably consider first of all a combination of split-shots to give me some idea of what my needs may be.

Other useful leger weights include first and foremost the Arlesey bomb, refined by Dick Walker from the pear-shaped lead in the early 1950s and endowed with a swivel to reach the perch at some distance, for which Bedfordshire's Arlesey Lake was to become noted. The bomb's torpedo shape permitted it to cut more cleanly through the air than other more conventional sinkers, and the swivel, while aiding the cast, also prevented the weight from entangling the line. The Arlesey bomb, having sorted out with flying colours the perch in the lake after which it was named, was then drummed into action for rolling a bait along the bottom of rivers and streams with equal success. It is now used frequently for all rigs demanding its special qualities, as well as some that don't, which must surely be the hallmark of a first-class legering lead.

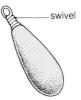

Figure 2 Arlesey bomb

Then there are the screw-bombs, developed as a direct result of the ban on lead which came into effect at the beginning of 1987. The screw-bombs come in various sizes and two parts, the

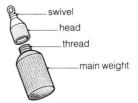

Figure 3 Screw-bomb

smaller of which stays on the line to receive the actual weight. It can be unscrewed in seconds to take another size. These I use regularly, and now wonder how I ever managed without them, so useful are they for all kinds of legering. There are various

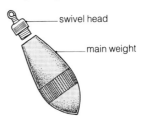

Figure 4 Dexter screw-bomb

designs such as the Dexter screw-bomb. Seymo bottle weights are another design brought about because of the lead ban, as are Dinsmores' Superbombs: similar to the Arlesey but not so finely streamlined. More on the specialist side perhaps are fluted weights, and most definitely for that scene is the buoyant leger from Middy. This is usually fished in conjunction with a paternoster, and keeps the hook-link above any offending weed on the bottom. And the latest Drennan weight (see below) makes all our lives easier!

Figure 5   Latest Drennan weight – lead unscrews from flexible stems to take different sizes

At first glance, then, it could be assumed we have quite a varied selection of weights to choose from, some of which are relatively new to us. Yet is that really the case? When compared with the vast variety of spinners and floats available, the choice of weights for legering at our disposal is and always has been somewhat limited, with scarcely more than three or four particular designs in regular use. So far, more thought seems to have gone into the different ways of rigging them up than into the invention of new-style leads. But angling has in modern times surmounted all hurdles, which is why it has advanced to the level of sophistication so evident now and, indeed, why during the last forty years its progress from a technical viewpoint at least has been a sight more influential than it ever was over the previous span of centuries. So the introduction of new lead designs is not, I trust, too far away.

Progress serves to demand yet more progress of every conceivable kind, and to allow the very means by which we put the bait amongst the fish on the bottom to languish, in a manner that is tantamount to our not caring a damn about it, is to presume that we care little about anything else – which is not the case, of course. Yet what a pity it would be if we quite suddenly came to a dead-end with all of our experimentation because the legering leads now at our disposal were found to be too archaic to warrant further thought as to how they might next be presented. For make no mistake, these are as much an intrinsic part of our entire set-up as everything else; a thought it might be as well to keep in mind.

Such is the situation at the present time, however, that I think the sinkers on offer are mostly ineffectual for our needs. This is why we continue to modernize those which we have, because almost without exception they're of little use to us as they stand and therefore require further attention to make them even half-way acceptable for our ever-increasing demands.

To elucidate further on the subject, let's look at a few leads from the past that are still very much with us today. Used these days mainly when the object is to fix the bait firmly on the bottom, the coffin lead was once nevertheless the most popular leger weight of all (probably because few really useful alternatives existed at the time). It also happened to be the worst possible lead of its kind for offering resistance to a taking fish, thanks to the pin-hole running through its centre for the line to

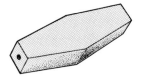

Figure 6   Coffin lead

go through. At the time of its creation the angler's thinking did not extend to such things as drag, which may explain why this poor excuse for a sinker managed to survive unchallenged for so many decades. And yet, strangely, it is still obtainable now, and should I by some horrible stroke of fate find myself with no option but to use this kind of sinker, then I'd quickly pass a short length of line through the middle, attach a split-ring or swivel to one end and a split-shot to the other to keep it in place and use it as a link-rig, which I'm sure would hold bottom nicely.

The ball or bullet lead can be used in the same way since it is defective in the same way as the coffin, and appears to have been around almost as long – and getting away with it too, which must surely lend weight to the remarks made above concerning our

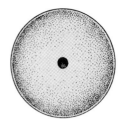

Figure 7   Pierced bullet or ball

cavalier attitude to this single segment of our terminal gear!

The barrel lead (occasionally known as the barleycorn) is also bad from the drag point of view – but at least it offers the least resistance to the air in casting when used as a running leger, and for this reason is chosen by some to add weight to a spinner, although our use of it as it stands is minimal since it again necessitates the incorporation of a link to justify for the better part its presence in our bag.

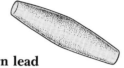

Figure 8   Barrel lead or Barleycorn lead

Now the Capta lead is something different again! A great deal of thought was expended on its design; no other lead even remotely resembles it. First appearing a decade or so after the last war it at least proved that someone somewhere at the time was thinking about leads. And yet despite this, the Capta has never been all that popular, which comes as something of a surprise. With a swivel attached (a necessity demanded more than ever now), it was designed to cause the least disturbance when hitting the water, an advantage about which a good deal

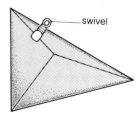

Figure 9   Capta lead

of fuss was made when the PR men got to work promoting the lead (which isn't cheap to buy, but then what leads are now?).

Its slightly out-of-accord pyramid shape also assures that it holds the bottom well, while at the same time, alas, making it a difficult lead to cast to any worthwhile distance; but then, you can't have everything I suppose!

The Catherine lead is less known than most but has its uses for all that. Its main claim to fame is that it is a quick-change slotted leger lead having a tapered and hollow plastic peg (also slotted) which passes right through the lead. The line goes

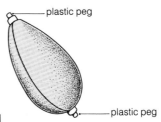

Figure 10   Catherine lead

through each slot and into the aperture of the peg, which is turned slightly to seal off the inner slot, after which the peg is pushed tightly home. The lead can now be moved up and down the line at will until stopped in the right place by a stop-knot, and is fairly resistance free in that it enables a bait to be taken and with it the line.

Finally there's the dear old pear-shaped sinker, with or without a swivel to which the line is attached. (Most definitely without in the bad old days of angling when any thought of the

Figure 11   Pear lead

finer points involved was sadly lacking in most!) Embedded in this sinker was a wire ring to which was tied the line, and generally it was reserved for paternostering, a method in which the weight played no part other than to act as a means to put out the bait and then to keep it there, most seductively off the bottom. Since the line didn't actually run through the lead the wire ring served its purpose well, and it was only when this and every other type of lead found itself being used as a running, rolling or link-leger that the need for a swivel or split-ring to make them the least resistant to a taking fish became more obvious to those who had finally reached the stage where such things concerned them more.

Designing and making your own sinkers

The mid 1950s and early 1960s saw, as in most things, a big boom in fishing. I like to think this was largely due to the continued success of the weekly publication *Angling Times* and its main contributor Dick Walker, who in some mysterious manner began to make anglers think for themselves. It was also a period which witnessed in *Angling Times*, and in a few other worthwhile angling publications of the time (notably the magazines *Fishing* and *Angling*, both now sadly long defunct), the emergence of not only a new breed of angler but one which was quite capable of putting thoughts into words.

From this new flow of blood pulsating through angling's veins, then, came many new theories and ideas based on the logical and sometimes scientific approach that we use today and which we could be pardoned for thinking had always been there. It took people such as Frank Guttfield, Peter Butler and others too numerous to mention here to put on their thinking caps and get down to some pretty basic, yet none the less highly concentrated research on our behalf.

Problems then, as now, were whittled away until the root of the matter was revealed and dealt with accordingly – and one of the biggest bugbears of that particular time was concerned with friction and the resistance felt by a taking fish. Tench were the *in* fish, and how to take them off a weedy or muddy bottom was the problem. This was eventually solved to some extent by the use of leger leads with an antenna attached through which the hook-link passed via a hole in the top to keep it above the offending weed and free of all resistance to the fish. The idea was simple and yet very effective, and readily available to everyone since the antenna was nothing more sophisticated than the inner section of a ball-point pen!

Rolling your own!

Not surprisingly, then, this encouraged others to experiment further and create all kinds of odd-ball sinkers to suit their own particular needs – most of which it must be said were soon jettisoned as those same needs, imaginary or otherwise, began to change – while those content to persevere with what was considered to be the norm of the day could make their own leads at home in one of the moulds that came on to the market at about that time. To be more inventive than that called for making your very own moulds – and what a messy business that was! Plaster of Paris was used for the moulds. When mixed it was ladled evenly into the trays of two matchboxes to take the impression of both sides of the leger weight to be forged. The plaster was then allowed to set, after which a hole was fashioned in one of the trays through which the molten lead was poured as the two halves of the mould were held together by one dubious means or another.

Not to be recommended for the young or inane (which makes me ponder on how I came to be messing about with it), 'rolling your own' as we called it was a dicey business at the best of times, and at the worst a decidedly dangerous one; and yet what fun we used to have, turning out sinkers the likes of which you'd never buy across the counter. I wonder why? It would seem, though, that I had a penchant for dreaming up weird if perhaps not-so-wonderful sinkers, and the fact of the matter is that I toyed with the idea of wrapping lead-wire around the bottom of the quill of a feather to keep my hook-link clear of weed (which worked very well, believe it or not) a good ten years before the suggestion of using the innards of a ball-point pen for the very same purpose was ever publicized in print, and probably nearly as many before it was even thought of.

This was followed up by a lead with an oval base that would sit upright on all but the most clinging of watery beds. From it protruded two (later reduced to one, to cut down on the friction factor) wire antennae to carry the hook-link well above any matter on the bottom that could foul-up the line running through a normal leger, and so cost me some fish. Why I didn't publicize or even market my invention I've no idea, unless it be because I thought such a move too preposterous for words just then. In any case, the celebrated Arlesey bomb arrived, which in one way or another served me well, so I eventually abandoned making my own leads altogether.

Indeed, it wasn't until I first went to Australia in 1965 that I was forced once again to make my own moulds and sinkers, Arlesey bombs and the like being unobtainable there. So out came the plaster of Paris once more! This time, though, I photographed proceedings, added around 500 words and sent the whole business off to a magazine called *Australian Outdoors*, and to the best of my knowledge it's *still* appearing in that publication's yearbook, which I reckon says a lot for 'rolling your own'.

4   Bite Detectors

Bite detectors have always fascinated me, not merely because without them we'd have no clear indication of a taking fish, and therefore little chance of connecting with it, but also, to be frank, because I get great fun from messing about with them; inventing them; adapting them fully to my own personal needs. Few things related to fishing please me more than finding an indicator that works just fine.

Quite obviously, like most other bits of gear, some work better than others in a given situation, and when the angler is concentrating on his fishing, and not day-dreaming a thousand worlds away, I have to say that again like most things the simplest detector is the best. I realized this some years ago, when reduced to catching some wily little wild trout on baits by watching the line where it entered the water, since all else in the way of bite detection had failed me, and so ridiculously simple was this method I couldn't understand why I hadn't tried it before.

But of course, tactics like this can succeed only in near-perfect conditions, and in a more general sense we need something a bit more practical – and that's where my main interest lies. And there have been literally dozens of weird and wonderful creations born for no purpose other than to tell us when there's a fish on the end of the line. What's more, most can be relied upon to this very day!

It seems strange, then, amidst the present mood of collecting and fishing with gear from way back, that when it comes to bite detection this interest in antiquity comes to an abrupt end. Strange indeed, when you consider how wrapped up in this old gear some anglers are; but you'll not catch many with a piece of silver foil on the line, it being all-electric bite buzzers these days

– which does, I feel, make something of a mockery of those who feign to live in angling's past.

As it happens, I once found myself in a situation where I had no choice but to turn the years back in order to fish even half-way effectively, and so I was glad of the previous experience I had had of using – and making – all manner of detectors, because I'd have been completely lost without them. And just thinking about them activated the brain cells again, not to mention my enthusiasm for such things, and that in turn led me to design a few more. Okay, when it comes to buzzers and the like my own efforts were not even in the running, but in the absence of such unique pieces of gear I was left to muddle through as best I could.

Now imagine, if you can, the effect that a piece of line hooked around a length of plastic curtain wire would have when pulled. That's right, the curtain wire would bend with it, and from that obvious bit of knowledge came a bite detector that worked quite well for me. Just an eighteen-inch strip of wire was first stuck into the ground, around which the line from the reel was placed after casting. Again the quarry was trout, and you should have seen how the wire bowed when a fish pulled, at which point the line slipped neatly off the end to leave it vibrating madly enough to catch the eye, which was an added bonus, of course.

From little acorns mighty oak trees grow. Not that anything quite that significant followed this first airing of the curtain-wire detector, although I did manage to develop it into something rather sophisticated, I thought, in spite of the knowing smiles that greeted it whenever it left my bag. For what I did was to shorten the length down to about five inches, place a metal washer at a point just below the tip to stop the line from sliding down it, and then set it in a 35 mm metal film container that was filled with lead to give it stability when on the ground.

Since the wire still vibrated so nicely I clipped the tiniest of bells to the tip which in action worked a treat, and, all things being taken into consideration, I was rather proud of that little gadget – not that I used it much because shortly afterwards angling writer George Walker, who originally hailed from the Midlands but now resides in South Australia, kindly sent me a

The coin-in-the-can detector

couple of home-made buzzers. But I did enjoy working on my bits and pieces of curtain wire because, as one bloke informed me, 'I've never seen anything like it!'

Other gadgets (or are they gimmicks?) have been less or more unbelievable, depending as much as anything else on your sense of humour, and yet they really did work. Take for instance the coin-in-the-can trick. Now that, to the best of my knowledge, was actually developed in the first place for carp fishing, no less, and sort of drifted over as usual into the general fishing scene. A coin (a two-bob bit [10p] was recommended in the first place because of its weight, but if you were that hard up then an old penny would have to do!) was placed on a stick across the mouth of a tin can under which the reel line lay, and when a fish took, the stick was thrown clear to let the coin drop in the can with such a thud it could be heard quite clearly on a still night. Now that's one means of detecting a take that I still use today, because it really is that reliable.

The cork bottle-stop detector came next, and was a natural progression I suppose from our old friend the dough bobbin, in that it was in itself a bobbin. A hair-clip was pushed right through the centre of the bottle-stop to secure it by a short length of line from the bend in the clip to a rod rest, while the main reel line was slipped between the two prongs of the clip projecting from the bobbin's other end. Affixed either between the reel and the first ring or hanging from the tip of the rod over the water, it was for a while a most idolized angling aid, until swing-tips, and then later quiver-tips, hit the marketplace with quite a bit of promotion behind them. After that the do-it-yourself types relented enough to let somebody else do it for them instead.

And so we had first the swing-tip and then the quiver-tip making inroads into a situation which really did need bringing

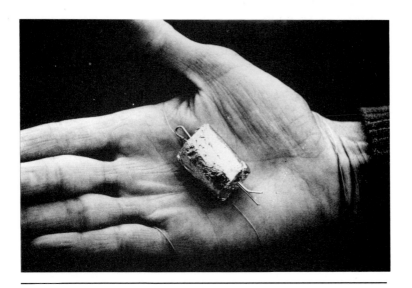

The cork bottle-stop detector, covered in silver-foil for night fishing

into line with other more progressive strides that were now beginning to affect angling in a more general sense. And just about then some thirty years ago, came into the shops the most ingenious bite detector of all: the Heron Bite Buzzer it was called, and some are still in use today (I have one myself, in fact, and am not above giving it an airing when the mood takes me). The Heron was a direct descendent of the electric buzzer conceived and used by Dick Walker in the capture of what is still the official British record rod-caught carp. The invention worked then and it works now. One of the biggest mistakes made in connection with the Heron, I think, was to use it in anything but still, or placidly flowing water. There were screws for adjusting the antenna to any flow, but in a decent flow it just didn't work effectively enough to win my respect.

The surest and most exciting way of detecting pulls in a fast, furious stream was and still is by feeling for 'em with the line wrapped around a finger in the touch-legering style. When that proved to be just too exhausting to continue without a break during a long, all-night session after barbel or chub (and believe me, there were nights like that, especially during the winter), I then reverted to the age-old idea of watching the top for bites with a strip of silver foil wrapped around it to catch any available light.

But that was before the betalight in its many guises appeared in the sixties, which was to some extent the answer to a night fisherman's prayer. Designed by Fred Buller and marketed by Hardy Brothers, they were known as Glow-bobbins from the very beginning, and contain a radioactive form of illumination that shows up well on even the darkest of nights.

And then at last came the now highly worshipped Optonic. No angler worth his salt would be seen dead on the bank without one, and not without good reason since they're sensitive enough to satisfy even the most fastidious among us, like me. But why do anglers continue to rob this wonderful creation of its true value by lumbering it up with grossly overweight bobbins for the fish to take up parallel with the rod?

Bobbins are fine in their place. In fact, if I had to use one or the other, I'd rather use a bobbin than a buzzer. I think the

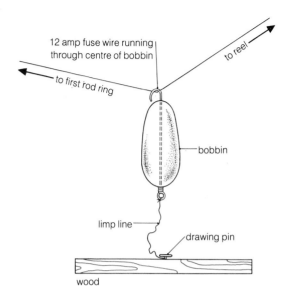

12 amp fuse wire running through centre of bobbin

to reel

to first rod ring

bobbin

limp line

drawing pin

wood

Figure 12 The balsa bobbin. The fuse wire straightens on strike to release bobbin from line

buzzer steals from the angler the thrilling visual effect of a take, unless used in conjunction with a bobbin, which it almost always is. But why add excess luggage for the fish to carry by way of the clumsy monkey-climbers and the like that I witness at the waterside so often? No wonder the whispered 'hesitant takers' are the norm these days, for what else can they be with all that hardware on the line to get moving? Sure, a hefty carp making off unsuspectingly with a bait in its mouth would have no trouble at all in smacking that bobbin hard up against the rod, but don't think for a minute that a delicately taking tench would be so obliging, because often it wouldn't – and I speak from painful experience here.

The bobbins I use are made of balsa, weigh about as much as a flea's earhole and have no hesitation whatsoever in informing me when to strike, not even when pretentious roach with delusions of being much-sought-after tench make off with the bait. Through each of my bobbins is threaded a short length of

12-amp fuse wire, fashioned into a hook at the top to take the reel line and twisted in a ring at the bottom to which is attached a section of light and very limp line which is secured by a drawing pin to a piece of wood on the ground. Now, when I strike, the fuse-wire hook straightens out and I'm left with nothing at all on the line to endanger further proceedings; while waiting there on the ground to be used over and over again is my bobbin, still pinned to that piece of wood. Simple. Then why clutter up your gear? Makes no sense at all to me.

Finally, I wonder what the future holds in store – or have we in the Optonic the ultimate weapon for detecting bites? Personally I doubt it, but in time we shall see. What I do believe will become a reality in the very near future are earplugs extending from the buzzers to convey the message that they're now operative. You may well be awoken in your bivvy one night to the tuneful chimes of 'Gone fishing, instead of just a-wishing'. So stir your stumps and make haste or all will be lost.

The balsa bobbin. The more advanced design is fitted with a fuse-wire hook (see Figure 12)

Buzzers

When Dick Walker caught Clarissa, his record-breaking 44 lb carp, on 12 September 1952, he certainly set the angling world ablaze. Yet whatever he did Dick simply couldn't do a thing right in some people's eyes – which is often the case concerning those who rise above the masses. Among the objections raised was his use of an electric buzzer. It allowed him to sleep, his critics cried, and so how can his approach be called fishing!

Few innovations have left their mark so vividly on the angling scene and, while there are still small pockets of resistance to the electric bite buzzer, the fact remains that few serious legermen are without them.

Walker's buzzer, one of the early designs, was a very basic arrangement by today's standards. It was activated when two contacts touched. They were kept apart by the reel line until a fish pulled it free, and it would continue to whine until switched off, having no further connection with whatever the fish did. It was a great boon to those fishing at night. Previously, nothing more sensitive had been available in the way of audible indicators than a bell affixed to a peg (or the faint rustling of a twist of silver paper being drawn across the grass in the dark, some would remind me). The night angler had been left to the dubious task of keeping his eyes fastened on a dough bobbin which would move in earnest more often than not only when he took his eyes from it for a second to light a cigarette or to put the kettle on the primus for a brew. At other times, as the hours crept by quite uneventfully, the bobbin would appear to do all manner of odd things – but that was just an illusion of course, the price paid for making do without sleep.

Yet still I delight in sitting there in the dark in just such a fashion: hoping, waiting and willing something to happen. On most occasions it does, I'm happy to say, which makes the entire ordeal of being on the night shift well worth while. Come the time now, though, when I see not just one bobbin on the line but two, or maybe even three, and I'll call upon the buzzers to take the strain and give my eyes a well-earned rest; not to allow me to continue fishing in my sleep, however (well, not often!)

Author gives his old buzzers a day out. Note also ultra-light balsa bobbins in use

but to let me relax a little and listen more profoundly to the voices of the night. While other means do exist to allow for as much, none has the reliability of the buzzer for jolting the angler out of his lethargy and back into the world of the living again, so that he can get on with the job.

It would be a mistake, though, to assume that such freedom naturally arrived with the first buzzer. Walker, when he set about inventing the original prototype, had big carp in mind, and while other fish may well have been quite capable of tugging the line free from the contacts to sound the alarm, there were those that were not; a state of affairs that still existed in my experience after the widely acclaimed Heron buzzer arrived around thirty years ago!

For fish the size of the average pike, for instance, they worked

Bite buzzers incorporated! Here are the Heron, the Beacon, Optonics and a pair of home-made jobs

a treat, but when it came to the likes of tench and bream the Heron didn't work half as effectively, and I'm sure many of these smaller species were lost to me because of the buzzer's lack of sensitivity. It was also fitted with an outrageously loud alarm (which I toned down a bit recently by applying some Blue-tac to the sound-box). But overall, as reluctant as I was to knock it – the Heron being most definitely a step in the right direction – I felt it was sadly lacking, as the development of more sophisticated electric bite buzzers was to prove.

The Beacon Bite Indicator, although working on much the same principle as the Heron by means of a fine adjustable antenna, was by way of weight, design and to a lesser degree sensitivity a vast improvement – so much so that it is still available on the market. But it came in as a very poor runner-up when the mighty Optonic entered the field of buzzers and began to dominate it in a way that left little doubt that the ultimate bite buzzer had arrived and intended to stay.

More research than ever had gone into the Optonic system which, briefly, is activated by a fish pulling the line over a roller. This in turn directs a minute fan blade to move across the field of a photo-electric cell to influence a beam of light within the buzzer's structure to react by producing a very noticeable audible sound, and to start winking in a most suggestive manner with its little red eye. Optonics are available as either compact models, which are completely self-contained within a single case, or as what are known as sensor heads, which are attached by leads to a communal sound-box and have buzzers of different tones described as Hi and Lo to let the angler know instantly which rod is clamouring for attention.

Since the invention of the Optonic, which as can be seen is completely unlike either the Heron or the Beacon buzzer but in effect supersedes them both to an amazing degree, others have attempted to come to the fore with varying levels of success.

Among the alternatives is the Bitech Viper Bite Alarm. This is sturdy in design and works by means of a wire cam as opposed to the Optonic's wheel. The audible tone can be varied on this equipment from a high-pitched whine to a deep thundery rumble, and the volume control can be adjusted to make it loud

To challenge the mighty Optonic is the new Bitech Viper Bite Buzzer

enough to wake the dead! Another interesting feature is the placing of both the indicating and latching LEDs. These protrude more fully than the Optonic's and can be easily seen when standing above the rod to put out groundbait, perhaps, which is just when the awkward cusses are most likely to make off with the bait! The V in which the rod is put to rest is unusually deep, adding to the security of it staying put in windy conditions (or perhaps when an extremely big fish tries to make off with it!), and the angle of this buzzer can be changed by a collar at its base to ensure that it always stands upright and proud. All of this makes the Bitech Viper a worthy contender for those with an eye peeled for something new to try.

5 Supporting the Rod

God only knows who first snapped a fork-shaped twig from a tree to rest his rod on, but that concept of a rod support has scarcely changed at all since then, only the materials from which it is forged. And having fished from a time when mass-produced rod rests were still a decade or so in the future, I have witnessed the introduction of them all (which is at least some compensation, I suppose, for being so long in the tooth!).

Yet even way back in the middle of the 1940s we kids became dissatisfied with a twig that was forever breaking as we tried to push the sharpened end firmly into the ground, and so what came next was a long piece of wood, supported at each end by whatever means we could muster on the bank to raise it just about six inches above the ground, on which all our rods were placed together after being cast out, their positions decided upon not so much by where each budding angler sat but rather more in line with where his terminal gear ended up in the water.

This in effect meant that for much of the time we were all stationed in readiness behind somebody else's rod, which we couldn't resist striking at, of course, when the dough-bobbin bounced to command our instantaneous attention. So in came the rule that whosoever struck at the fish should also bring it in, since nobody could fairly claim it if one hooked the fish and then handed the rod over to its rightful owner.

Surprisingly, this arrangement worked perfectly well, with never a disagreement as I remember, although one of our number keener than most did have the good fortune to be almost always in the right place at just the right time until it was noticed that he shifted his bum around a lot more than most, and that's when our mutual rod rest was itself laid to rest. Not that I could in retrospect apportion much blame to him for that, since he was even at that early age quite obviously a fishing freak who was prepared to go to any lengths to succeed. He was also to be the last remaining member of our group with whom I continued to fish right up until we both found ourselves doing our (very little) bit for Queen and country.

After demobilization we met up again to carry on exactly where we'd left off and, as fate would have it, we both quite independently found ourselves in Australia and managed to fish together on occasion there also, despite a distance of almost 500 miles separating us. Since we first met on a train returning from a fishing trip when he was an eleven-year-old and I was all of twelve, I deem that the kind of friendship to be proud of.

It wasn't long after we dispensed with our community rod rest that more purpose-built ones began to drift on to the market, but these were heavy beyond words. The fishing tackle manufacturers Efgeeco then got into the act by bringing out on a mass-produced basis the kind of rubber rod-rest tops which are still so fashionable today. If treated roughly they were apt to snap, but they were cheap enough to replace without further thought and, when pushed on to a metal or even stout wooden rod, they were and still are the best means for supporting the angler's rod. In design they allow for the passage of the line beneath the rod, an absolute necessity for those concerned with sensitivity to a taking fish.

Since then, however, we've seen the arrival of two-piece extending rod supports and a neat little arrangement put out by the East Anglian Rod Co. Ltd known as the Swing Rod-Rest, which in practice remains vertical irrespective of the angle at which the bank stick goes into the ground. And, of course, we also have the buzzer bar. Now this is fine if both rods are pointed in the same direction and not too much wind is blowing, but for those who insist on having their entire gear from bait to reel in a straight line, with one rod perhaps slanted to a sheltered shallow on the left and another to a shelf below the surface to the right, buzzer bars can prove to be more of a hindrance than an asset.

As great as they are on many occasions, buzzer bars should never be thought of as the final solution to supporting one's

All set and ready to go. The trouble with buzzer bars is that they restrict the angle at which two rods can be used

rods. Often, completely independent front and rear rod rests do a far better job without any extra support to keep them steady in the wind. I suspect that one reason some people now avoid the latter like the plague is that buzzer bars are more fashionable; also some anglers may have difficulty in managing without the monkey-climbers and needle stands so closely associated with these bars.

It seems to me that the angler with a comprehensive selection of rod rests to choose from must invariably get it right, and by knowing exactly what he needs beforehand will nip in the bud the frustrating business of finding he's got it all wrong when at the water and too late to do much about it. And believe me, having the rod set up correctly and comfortably is of no less importance than all the other paraphernalia we strive to get right, for it all combines to make our approach as foolproof as we can possibly get it.

However little the subject of rod supports is discussed in the angling press, there are those among us who appear to think about nothing else. This much I was to learn back in 1964 when an article of mine entitled 'Rod Rests Really Do Matter' was published in the then weekly magazine *Fishing*. The topic caught the imagination of readers and contributors alike, and continued to be debated for months on end in print to a degree that was quite without parallel in the publication before or since as far as I know. As I've said, it is imperative to extend the same meticulous care to the matter of rod supports as to the remainder of your preparation. In order to strike quickly at a rapid bite it is necessary to have all the relevant factors in harmony before ever wetting a line.

There's room for compromise and initiative, too, of course – when fishing from a concrete foundation, for instance, when you can't force a rod rest into the ground. Try boring a hole into a hefty wooden block in which the rod rest can stand upright and firm.

What I'm still waiting to see developed is a one-piece support that takes the weight of the rod from behind the reel where the normal rear rod rest would go, and has an arm extending to the first runner perhaps to steady the remainder of the rod. It would be simple yet, I believe, very effective.

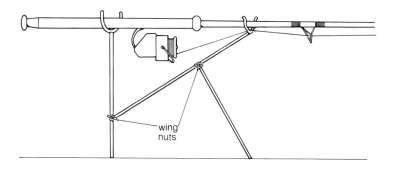

Figure 13　Suggested rod rest design

6   Hook Review

It has been said earlier, and on good authority I might add, that man has eaten fish since he first stood on two legs and discovered that he could do more with his hands than just walk on them to get from A to B. Indeed, when Dr L.S.B. Leakey, a prominent British anthropologist, excavated a deep chasm in Tanzania in central Africa, he uncovered not only the skeletal remains of an ancient tribe described as being ape-like men who walked upright (*Australopithenes*) and who may well have been an earlier version of true man (*homo*), but also, and more to the point, some remains of the food he ate at the time, including fish, which scientists claim to be 1·8 million years old.

Therefore it seems safe to assume that man has fished in one way or another since the first awakening of his history, and that after dabbling with first his bare hands and then forked or pointed sticks, to be followed by traps with which to ensnare the catch, he finally turned to the fishing hook, which was almost certainly made of wood. This is borne out by the fact that a branch with twigs attached at a convenient angle would lend itself most fittingly to the task of catching fish, however impossible such an approach would seem to us today. Even the thorns of a hawthorn bush have been used as hooks in the past, with considerable success, as have hooks fashioned from shells, the beak of an eagle and the claw of a hawk. As late as the last century human jawbones were shaped into fish hooks by one particular tribe, which illustrates just how desperate the situation can get for some!

From the late Palaeolithic period, hooks for fishing were made from bone. But before that, hooks were made out of wood, although gorges might be a better word to describe them since, initially, to use them as such was the aim. It is also interesting to note that Hans Jorgen Hurum suggests in his book *A History of the Fish Hook**: 'Since wood floats, the hook would probably have to be fastened to a stone or something else that was heavy enough to make it sink.' And if that cannot be described as legering, no matter how primitive, then I don't know what can; all of which is proof enough, by my reckoning, that the idea of legering a bait on the bottom has been there since primeval time.

From that time on the development of the fish hook seems to have been a very long drawn-out process; it took literally thousands of years for barbs to appear on them but just a fraction of that time, it now seems, for them to start disappearing again. And to think I blamed the absence of a barb for failing to catch on a bent pin when a boy! But until the end of the Middle Ages, making do with what you could knock up yourself was the only way to kit yourself out for the sport – not that it was widely considered as such then, which probably goes a long way in explaining why barbs took such an inordinate amount of time to catch on. But at about this time blacksmiths were busy turning out hooks on a commercial level for professional fishermen.

Dame Juliana Berners came on to the scene then, by saying in *The Treatyse of Fyshinge wyth an Angle* (1496) that the best hooks were made from needles – the finest darning needles preferably for small fish, embroidery needles for those a bit bigger and finally a tailor's or shoemaker's needle for the whoppers that always get away. From there progress eventually reached the stage where hook-making on a professional level was no longer a cottage industry, with people such as Charles Kirby turning out hooks in London as early as the 1600s. Among other famous names connected with the fishing-hook industry at various times since then are Allcock, Sealey, Mustad, Milward, Drennan, and later after the Japanese tackle invasion Kamasan, which unless I'm mistaken was the first to bring us chemically-sharpened hooks. So today we are in the agreeable situation of having a huge selection of hooks available to choose from.

*Kindly sent to me by E.R. Sarbutts of Mustad & Son Ltd

Mustad, for instance, have been producing hooks for a worldwide market at their factory in the tiny township of Gjovik, on the banks of Lake Mjosa, southern Norway, for over a century now, during which time the company has produced 103,800 different varieties of fish hooks, each of which had some unique feature, be it of size, colour, material or shape, and 60,000 of these have at one time or another been obtainable from across the tackle dealer's counter.

7   Legering Lines

How those anglers of old ever got by on lines made of horsehair is indeed puzzling, for hair (horses' or otherwise) isn't exactly known for its strength unless it just happened to belong to Samson. And yet somehow they managed to bring in fish the likes of which we wouldn't object to today.

Thinking about it leads me to feel just a little bit better about the thread-like Cuttyhunk line that I was obliged to persevere with when a boy. It was customary then to grease one's line before each outing, having first wound it around the back of a chair. Candle wax was recommended, but I was aghast at how easily my 12-lb line busted after being treated in this fashion, probably because I hadn't taken proper care to dry it after my last fishing trip.

I was about twelve or thirteen years of age at the time, and I can't help thinking about how fortunate young anglers are today to have the kind of lines I wouldn't have dared even to dream about when I was a boy. Those same thick and incredibly heavy lines that I had to make do with when their age had to be cast by laying them out on the ground. Yet I don't regret it in the least. It gave me the kind of foundation for angling that doesn't exist any longer, and for that I'll always be grateful.

Nylon monofilament line, when it finally arrived, was still for all practicable purposes out of our reach, and when we did eventually begin to get our grubby little hands on some it was in short lengths only, of no more than 25 yards. But how great it was just to lie the line at our feet and cast without fear of a tangle; and how easily any that did occur were pulled free again in no time at all. This was the stuff that dreams were made of to us. It made a big difference to our fishing, I can tell you.

Since then, of course, we've all come to take for granted the enormous range of options open to us when selecting a new spool of line. And yet is the choice really that great? Apparently not. In fact, it seems that only a few large chemical companies produce the fishing lines that we use, which then go out to smaller concerns with a different label attached. Therefore, unless we're wary of such things we may well change our brand of line but finish up with the same as we already had.

Sylcast and Maxima are well known brands. Both are immensely popular, and I've always found them very reliable, while Drennan's double-strength has brought a new dimension into the business of fishing lines by giving us pound for pound a product which is only half the diameter of other lines of comparable strength. This in effect means we're now fishing with a line that appears to be five pounds test, for instance, when in fact it has the strength of a ten-pound line – and it seems to me there's a lot to be gained from that, providing anglers can adapt. But we are of course, creatures of habit and will undoubtedly continue to use old favourites when it comes to line simply because they have earned our trust.

There are characteristics other than the thickness and strength of line to be looked at, however. I have always considered colour to be important, if only for the reason that if it doesn't look right then I don't feel right using it. I'm a firm believer in the maxim that to succeed one must have total confidence in every aspect of the gear, and that includes lines! Indeed, it wasn't too long ago that the accepted practice of specimen hunters, at least, was to dye their lines and paint their leads to blend in with the bottom of the water. If fishing over a bed of mud, for instance, the line would inevitably be black, green when the bottom was covered in weed, and so on, which was said to do no harm to the angler's chances of contacting a big fish and might well add to them a great deal. This is also true of many other little points which singularly might not perhaps represent much of a benefit at all, but added together become something else again. That was how Dick Walker used to look at it, and who am I to disagree?

There was also a time when the most natural thing in the world was to buy hooks already whipped to very fine nylon, and these worked well enough for years. The whipping did have a tendency to fray after continuous use, but I never knew it to come undone. These became unfashionable when the conclusion was arrived at that knots in the terminal end of the gear represented a weak link, and so we all went through the motions of tying eyed hooks and later spade-end hooks directly to the reel line ourselves. Spade-ends I eventually gave up on after losing two decent barbel in the space of one night due to the knot slipping. Since I'd tied those knots their failure to hold was obviously down to me, but the experience shattered my confidence in my own tying and it took a long time to be renewed.

These days, although many people still have more confidence in their own tying than they have in commercial tyers, tying hooks directly to the reel line is no longer acceptable in much of the specialist scene, where the leaning now is definitely towards more subtle hook-links again. Supple might be a better word to use since most brands of nylon monofilament are now thought to be too coarse and stiff to be fished in close proximity to the fish. Materials like dental floss and braided terylene are being used on which to tie the hook. Dental floss unravels when wet to become multiple strands that are less likely to spook the fish. These are known as 'soft' hook-links. Soft fibres are now spooled and sold for the sole purpose of making hook-links, and if you're wondering why all these changes are now deemed necessary, I can offer two reasons. The first is that the fish are learning faster than we are now, due to the increased pressure to catch them. The second I believe rests firmly at our own door, for whether or not we require it the search continues unabated for perfection, and to my mind that's no bad thing.

8 The Legered Bait

Most anglers hinge their chances of battling to a standstill some leviathan of the deep on a single, or at best just two kinds of bait. This has always been the case, from the days when nothing but a big helping of bread paste or flake on the hook would be considered good enough for bream, until now, when boilies alone will catch carp, or so we've been led to believe. It can be quite confusing at times when trying to understand why this preoccupation with a specific bait exists. For ringing the changes in respect to baits, more so than any other single factor I would venture to say, is often the short-cut to the success that many anglers dream about. The bigger the selection we have to choose from the less likely we are to be stumped when the fish are fed-

Old fashioned bait can (*Ray Cannon Collection*)

A beautiful stretch of the Dorset Stour, where barbel appeared at one time to be almost impossible to catch

up to the eyeballs with what we have on the hook.

Baits, like everything else connected with fishing, are apt to drift in and out of fashion at will; which would be puzzling but for our awareness of just how short-lived some baits are in respect to their effectiveness – which makes it all the more surprising that some anglers are loath to change their regular baits in favour of another that just might pay better dividends.

On my tench water I have done very well with sweetcorn. Corn was the popular bait long before I got there and as such is now frowned upon as being blown. Blown my eye! I'm still reaping a damned good harvest with it, and attribute that a great deal to the fact that I'm one of the few on the water still persevering with it!

I recall during the early sixties trying to reduce the barbel of the Troop Fisheries stretch of the Dorset Stour on maggots, cheese and worm, and not a single fish did I deceive into making my fortnight-long assault on them even remotely worth while.

But at the time I wasn't alone in my failure, because nobody then experienced continuous success, and any fish taken at all on Troop at that particular time was akin to winning the pools! Yet now barbel are to be had quite frequently, on maggots as much as anything else, which raises the question, of course, as to why they shunned the bait in the first place? It was supposed at the time that the abundance of natural food in the river fed the barbel well enough without them resorting to something which they didn't expect to find. But of course, far more anglers fish the water now, more often than not with maggots, and so it seems to me the fish have come to accept them on the river bed as a part of their natural diet.

Wheat was a popular bait during my boyhood, then after the war it was superseded by hemp. And what fine roach my father began to pull out on it from the Thames, the likes of which I had previously never even suspected of existing in the swims we had fished for years. Now, albeit hesitantly, wheat is making something of a come-back, although not so elderberries it would seem, which were at one time almost as popular as wheat used to be.

Cherries are another neglected bait for chub, which adore them almost as much as I do. I was taught a lesson in taking chub from the weirs on cherries a long time ago. Exciting stuff it was, and a most welcome change from the usual methods of chub fishing. One didn't use a sinker but just cast the cherry on a free line and worked it down to the fish – and it hardly ever travelled that deeply without a good fish intercepting it. But perhaps we're stretching the credibility of legering a bit too far here, although cherries have accounted for chub when fished right on the bottom too, and when all else seems doomed to failure cherries are a possibility to keep in mind.

If there's one bait I would choose above all others when the pressure is really on, though, it would have to be worm. By that I don't mean a sickly brandling, or a twiggy-type red worm, but a big and lively lobworm that's just burrowed its way to the top of the lawn at night. They can, of course, be turned over with a spade, but somehow these seem inferior in both firmness and movement when compared with those taken from the lawn at night, and I discovered long ago that a meaty lobworm or two on the hook was liable to score with at least some species when other baits remained untouched by the fish. But naturally, much would depend on the conditions faced. Try a lob in the middle of a dry summer day, for instance, and you couldn't expect it to produce the goods, but at night, when the temperatures start to fall, what a different story we have to tell then. So it's all down to sensible application again.

Don't forget, either, that there's not a single fresh water fish that won't at some time take a worm; and that goes for old *Esox lucius* also. Much the same can be said of the maggot, on which I've had quite a few pike lately, which makes me wonder what on earth is happening to the so-called 'freshwater tiger' to make it take puny baits like that. What we have in the maggot is yet another bait of addiction – so much so that some anglers never use anything else, despite the fact that it is largely a very inferior bait, suitable only for weenies for most of the time. Yet reluctant though I am to admit as much, maggots when used in bulk (and I do mean in bulk) have accounted for some very nice fish, especially barbel, although who's to say that the same results wouldn't have been achieved eventually if some other bait had been stock-piled on the river bed?

The idea of conditioning the fish to accept a bait as normal by introducing mountains of it is by no means a modern manoeuvre. Thames barbel fishers of old were well noted for the thousand upon thousand of lobworms they put into the water to encourage the fish to feed. However, nowhere have I read anything to suggest that their pre-baiting with worms had an adverse affect on those wishing to fish with another bait – which is very much the case when gallons of maggots are left to litter the river's bed. This at one time caused the bait to be banned on the Royalty Fishery at Christchurch, because the fish came to look at nothing else. But when those smitten by the maggot mania stayed away in droves, the powers that be relented and back they came in force, to tackle the fish in the Hampshire Avon in the only way they knew how, while at the same time spoiling the chances of those with a bit more imagination and doubtless a lot more skill, plus a sight more interest in the sport that called for something more varied on the hook. That's the way it was on the Avon before the maggot invasion took place.

As for casters (which I grew up to know as chrysalids), there was a time when I'd dispose of these as having no further use; until, that is, the day I met an ageing angler on the banks of the lower Thames at Hampton Court. I was probably about fourteen at the time, and therefore with an unquenchable thirst for knowledge, so I watched with open mouth all that this old-timer did with a biscuit-tin full of casters. 'I bet you usually throw chrysalids away?' he asked, reeling in one nice roach or dace after another, and all I could do was nod my head like an imbecile, after which I bought a whole pint of maggots and couldn't wait for them to change into deadly chrysalids.

It's sad to relate here, though, that I obviously waited a mite too long; and how unpopular I became at home when, removing the lid from the tin my fantastic new bait was kept in, the house was filled with flies. You can be sure that after that frightening experience I made a practice of putting the tin to an ear before opening it to ensure that nothing inside buzzed!

I was also fortunate enough to be on the scene when sausages as bait became all the rage; and what fun we all had then, trying to keep it on the hook. Only by par-boiling the bait before use did any of us solve that little problem, although I personally turned to chipolatas in the end, which proved to be less expensive and far more inclined to stay on the hook without any preparation whatsoever, and the barbel and chub loved them. Sausages and chipolatas have now been replaced by luncheon meat, (but only the best brand, mind, and nothing at all like we have in our sandwiches!).

Bread paste, crust or flake will always be around as choice bait; no matter what becomes trendy for a time, bread will be lurking in the background like the good trooper it is, waiting to be called to battle stations again. Dick Walker showed us all just how adaptable a piece of bread can be by utilizing the properties of both crust and paste together to form a 'balanced' bait that would sink slowly to the bottom, and once there rest gently upon any weed present. From Redmire he caught his

**The Royalty Fishery on the Hampshire Avon, prior to the
days when the bed of the river became riddled with maggots**

record carp on it, making redundant any further need for
qualification. During the first few weeks of the season I still
favour bread paste above all other baits for tench, and it's still
not to be dismissed as an offering for big bream at that time of
year, either, although whether carp are still susceptible to it or
not is difficult to find out now that boilies reign supreme on that
scene.

At the initial introduction of boilies, which are egg based and
flavoured with God knows what, a great tidal wave of relief must
have swept over those plagued with the age-old problem of how
to avoid uninvited intruders from taking the bait. For as carp
anglers learned very quickly when huge helpings of paste were
more in favour than they are these days, neither the tench nor
the bream could resist such a mouthful, no matter how big, just

The ultimate big perch bait – a smaller version of its own kind

as the barbel and chub men were to discover about roach and dace, which on occasion took their lobworms or cheese cubes with glee. It was for this very reason that boilies came into being: to defeat other species with dishonourable designs on the carp angler's baits.

However, it's no secret that to most would-be big carp conquerors, boilies became quite suddenly irreplaceable, and the novice angler today could be excused for thinking that there never had been any other kind of bait for carp. What exceptions there are to this come in the form of tiger nuts, peanuts and a few other carefully selected nuts, but boilies are by far a more widely used bait. Blessed with more flavourings than space will allow for here, the object is to find another as soon as those currently in use begin to lose their appeal to the fish, and so the search continues for yet another new flavour – there appearing, on the surface at least, to be precious little time in which to test the full potential of each.

Mussels are a very unrecognized bait, but serve well for many species including tench and trout

Small fish are not used often enough for bait, either; and by that I don't mean merely for pike, perch or eels, but rather more for fish like barbel and chub, and perhaps even carp, tench and bream. For the reality of the issue is that all species will at times devour small live and dead fish. Anyone who keeps an aquarium will know that much.

I recall a time when members of the old Barbel Catchers' Club toyed with the idea of using elvers for bait. Portions of lamprey had in the past been hailed as such a fine barbel bait, and elvers were the nearest we could get to these at that time. To be able to say we succeeded beyond our wildest dreams would be nice, but the fact is we encountered a problem that wasn't even thought of before. 'How do you kill the bloody things?' asked the late Peter Mead, resigned to the certain knowledge that it was not possible to keep a live one on the hook. Since we discovered no sure way of killing them the entire idea was dismissed as being too impracticable. I have often wondered, though, how well we might have fared had we managed in some way to fish elvers for barbel. If anybody has achieved as much will they please let me know.

One might also be advised to try taking a leaf from the fly fisher's book. There are no end of possible baits, ranging in size from the smallest insect you can reasonably be expected to stick on a leger hook to the kind of large creepy-crawly you wouldn't normally dare touch with the proverbial barge-pole. (It's surprising what we will touch, though, when in desperate need of some baits!) A whole new world is open to the angler prepared to experiment here, and to adapt his approach in a manner he has never been called upon even to think about before.

Groundbaiting

Groundbaiting is at the best of times a bit tricky; at the worst it can be downright suicidal and completely ruin your sport, as it once did mine. This happened at a time when there were bream aplenty in those vast sheets of water known as the Norfolk Broads, and yet after a string of successful visits to the water I unaccountably blanked, and decided afterwards that the most obvious reason for this was my groundbait which at the tail end of the week-long session could have smelt and tasted, I dare say, a lot better. So in practice all I succeeded in doing was scaring the fish right out of the swim with my obnoxious, evil-smelling feed, and I have been wary of such things ever since.

Groundbait, I had learnt to my cost, needs to be prepared with the same consideration and thought as everything else. These days it's more likely to consist of particle baits by the bucketful rather than the old, bulky mixture of bread and bran together with a little of what you fancied in the way of hook bait to give it that extra appeal.

Additives are now more or less in general use to enhance the attraction of groundbait as well as the hook bait, and they come in a variety of flavours, Bloodworm and Tubifex being two extremely popular offerings from the Ultimate Angling Additive range, with the promise of more to come. But again we've nothing new! Bread paste mixed with honey goes way, way back, to long before even I was born; and I clearly remember some very big carp taken from the notoriously hard Billing Aquadrome Water on banana-flavoured paste at least thirty years ago, when such fish were still rare enough to cause quite a stir in angling circles.

Secret formulas were whispered about even then, containing as they did such supposedly illegal ingredients as aniseed and the roe of a salmon. There was also talk about the adverse effect the drug-like qualities of hempseed had on the fish, because it soon became apparent that on occasion roach especially just couldn't resist this witches' brew, and often, in place of the piece of valve rubber that was used so spectacularly to trick the roach into thinking it was hemp, I'd tempt them with nothing but a split-shot on the hook, so aroused were they by the seed. But how appalled I was when boiling a roach or two for the cat (a common enough practice in those days) to find the saucepan literally filled to the brim with hemp, giving me reason enough to question the wisdom of using it even then, when just a sprinkling of hemp around the float was the order of the day. What the situation might be at present, with entire carpets of the stuff put down to attract the fish, I dread to think.

I am a firm believer in trying to keep every aspect of the sport on as elementary a base as current conditions allow. It's extremely challenging as it is, I reckon, without adding complexities to it which can only serve to cloud the issue even further for the beginner, who has enough to contend with during his initiation period without worrying unduly about additives and the like. There will be time enough for that as his proficiency grows.

However, being the impatient lot that we are (blessed not with mindless patience but controlled impatience, was how Dick Walker once described it), we're bound to think in serious terms about the use of additives simply because we know they are there.

Precise instructions usually come with pre-packed additives, which should be followed with care. And I would further suggest that when using additives for the first few times you should err on the side of caution, and any qualms at all arising out of their use be given the benefit of the doubt. Far better that than to blow your chances completely by carrying on regardless in a situation which is completely unknown to you. With experience those doubts will begin to diminish as your confidence with additives grows.

Having reached that delightful pinnacle it's time to turn to the task of getting the groundbait out to the fish, and there's been no shortage of inventive minds at work here resulting in several options for carrying out this manoeuvre, the most popular of which is undeniably the swim feeder, which is dealt with more fully in the next section. Bait-droppers are somewhat similar, and offer us another means of putting the feed perhaps not quite where we need it, a point I was forced to acknowledge years ago when determined to sort out in no uncertain terms the barbel which lived in a lower Thames weirpool.

Monsters they were not, but fought well enough to the net despite their size, and on one particular occasion I bought a bait-dropper especially for the purpose of littering the bed with maggots in order to get the barbel on the move. But, oh dear, what a farce that proved to be! Where the maggots eventually finished up I've no idea, but wherever it was the barbel went along too – or that's the excuse I used for catching nothing at all that night!

Getting maggots and the like down to the fish in fast water is a challenge in itself, especially when some distance is to be attained. A catapult is just the tool for the job, providing it's not called upon to tackle a heavy flow, in which case loose maggots will be swept down with the stream. Maggots embedded in firm balls of groundbait or earth should do the job then.

Marketed by Enak, Dissolvo Bait Bags give the angler another choice for baiting up the swim with the least possible effort. This can be done speedily and accurately with Dissolvo bags, because all that is required is for the bait to be placed in the bag, a stone added to sink it to the bottom and the neck sealed with a damp finger. Once on the river bed, of course, the bag dissolves within thirty seconds or so to leave the feed where the fish will find it.

Soluble tape (which is also put out by Enak) has been around for years, but these bait bags are something relatively new, although Fred Buller introduced soluble bait bags as a carrier for groundbait bombs twenty-five years ago. They were made from Polyvinyl Acetate and were marketed by Martin James Ltd. The idea sprang from a method of introducing chemicals into sheep dip! I have seen nothing else quite like the Dissolvo bags. I've used them not only for maggots, hempseed and corn but also for lively lobworms, which previously presented something of a problem when it came to getting them on the bottom in the right place.

From this latest development let's look, however briefly, at a few old do-it-yourself groundbait dispensers which have survived the ravages of time. The most basic of these is the leger lead itself, to which is moulded bread of the correct consistency to make it stay put during the cast and yet break loose with a gentle jerk of the rod top to leave it as an attractor on the river bed. A coil of spring-wire on the line which carried the bread in much the same way as the lead was another dodge used; as was a weighted Coca-Cola can with holes punched in it to allow the maggots to flee. But surely the simplest and therefore most effective of all was the idea of letting nature do the groundbaiting for us. This was accomplished by merely tying a dead bird or animal to the branch of a tree jutting out over the swim to be fished later, and allowing the flies to complete the task by ensuring that within a matter of days a steady trickle of maggots fell into the water to bring the fish around. Now if there is an easier and less time-consuming way of feeding the swim than this, I've yet to hear about it.

Feeder fishing

Cylindrical in shape and made from perforated perspex, swim feeders are unique in concept in that they deposit feed and groundbait right where it is needed most, i.e. in close proximity to the baited hook. Yet however modern and sophisticated such advanced thinking may seem to be on the surface, the fact of the matter is that swim feeders first made an appearance centuries ago, when they weren't all that dissimilar to those we

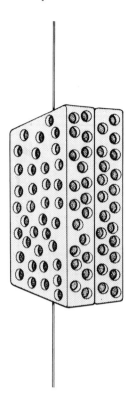

Figure 14   Old fashioned swim feeder

use today. They were containers with holes punched in them to allow the bait to flee the coop. One can only imagine that tiny tin pill boxes with tightly fitting lids were used for the purpose, as were actually described in *The Gentleman's Recreation* by one Nicholas Cox – in 1674!

Swim feeders have since re-emerged and disappeared again on several occasions. But return they always do and so have gained a niche almost unprecedented in the annals of angling history. Intended mainly for big fish at their conception, swim feeders eventually invaded the bags of the pleasure angler as well as the match angler, to the point where few these days would be caught napping without at least a few different samples and sizes in their tackle bags. But in reality that's just half of the story!

Swim-feeder fishing grew to become more widely known simply as feeder fishing, which is how the situation stands today. It has, over the years, been developed into a very fine art, combining as it does its own means of bite detection as well as rods designed for the sole purpose of fishing the feeder. These have a tendency to be quite powerful overall, but with a more forgiving tip than normal to allow for the lighter lines often associated with feeder tactics, without which the sudden wrench of finding a weighty feeder on the end would break the line with the least prompting, unless a shock-leader of heavier line than the main reel line is used. This has solved the problem for some, but not all anglers it must be said, some of whom still commit swim feeders to the murky depths as their line snaps with monotonous regularity.

Making contact with the fish instead of the feeder on striking might also be a doubtful business without that bit of extra pulling power in the rod. Some purpose-built feeder rods also incorporate quiver-tips to serve as the main means of detecting a fish at the bait, although there has lately been a noticeable return to the less flexible swing-tips in some areas – another example of how fluctuating is our acceptance of such things.

The swim feeders themselves come in several shapes and sizes, known respectively as open-ended and block-end feeders – the former being used mainly for bread or cereal-based groundbait and the latter for maggots and the like. A strip of lead or a couple of swan-shots usually act as the weight to take them out to the required distance and down to the fish, and either a swivel, split-ring or nylon loop is used to attach them to the line, sometimes with a boom of silicone tubing or something similar in place to minimalize the chance of a tangle whilst casting. Perhaps this effectively turns the rig into a link-leger. As always, someone somewhere will be busily creating his own swim feeders to ensure that some variations from the so-called norm are forever in existence.

But what now is the norm? Swim feeders are beginning to change in appearance as well as in concept, making the ugly and positively clumsy contraptions that first put me off them redundant. Peter Drennan, long-time confederate of Oxford maestro Peter Stone, was the first as far as I know to tidy up the image of swim feeders in order to give us an option with a little more thought and design behind it, after which other manufacturers were quick to follow suit.

Daiwa have since brought out Harrier feeders, which not only rise from the bottom on the retrieve to avoid snagging but also offer less of a handicap when playing a fish. Previously the resistance offered by swim feeders generally tended to take much of the fun out of the fight.

The feeders with interchangeable clip-on weights, put on the market by Henry Aiken, would have represented a most innovative move had this same versatility not been already available to us in the form of Drennan feeders weighted by swan-shot which could be added or subtracted when the need arose. But that is not to say that there wasn't room for further experiment along these lines, for there always will be as long as anglers and tackle manufacturers can put their heads together for the good of us all. Aiken are to be commended for giving us an alternative to what was already available. Varitech Tools

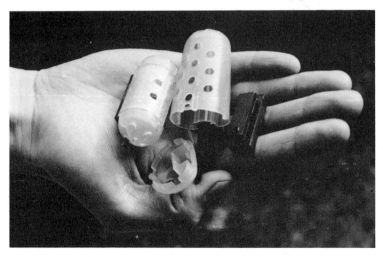

Popshot swim feeders, with quick-change heavy plastic weights

Ltd must also take a bow for their Popshot Swim Feeder, which embraces its own interchangeable weight system. In design its aerodynamic shape is intended to stabilize the feeder on the bottom in the worst conditions, and the weights, which ingeniously just slot into place, are made from non-toxic heavy plastic, a hint perhaps of what the future holds in the way of weighting feeders.

And now we also have cage feeders, offered by the East Anglian Rod Company as well as other manufacturers. These open-enders of wire mesh offer next to nothing in the way of resistance to the water when being wound in, which is their main advantage. Being skeletal in design they permit groundbait to be deposited on the bottom and amongst the feeding fish with the least delay. Other feeders can carry their weight inside of them, or suspended at the base by a nylon link running through the interior of the feeder and attached to the reel line by a swivel at the other end, and the list doesn't end there. So, what comes next – jet-propelled swim feeders? Not quite.

But how about spring-loaded feeders? The aptly named Auto

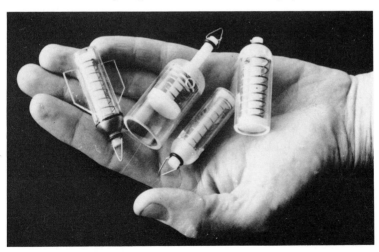

Spring-loaded auto swim feeders. Note the fins on the moving water model to stop it rolling

Swim Feeders, available from the company of Griffin, in Cheshire, are exactly that – spring-loaded; and I foresee something of a future for these. In practice, a coiled spring inside the feeder is pulled back while it is loaded and the contents held in place by the usual plug of groundbait or mud. Made to the right consistency (five parts to one part of water is the manufacturer's recommendation) the plug holding back the spring will soften and the latter will eject the feed within a minute and a half after casting – 'While standard swim feeders will still be full!' promises the promotional literature and I find no reason to disagree with that. The still-water variety are unweighted, while those intended for moving water are not only weighted but also fitted with fins to stop them rolling on the bottom. An ingenious idea all round!

Originally designed to sit tightly on the bottom, swim feeders are now used in roving tactics as well, particularly on the bigger rivers such as the Trent and the Thames, where it was discovered that drifting a meticulously weighted feeder slowly along the bottom sent the chub into feeding frenzies the likes of which at times seemed quite unparalleled by anything from the past. This is understandably a pretty tricky business, however, better left to the expert rather than to the beginner, who is best advised to let his feeder settle on the bottom and allow the feed trickling from it to bring the fish to him instead.

Light lines and tiny hooks are normally the order of the day, with block-end feeders at least, which should contain a fair portion of whatever is on the hook – usually maggots. And since the bait is correspondingly small, so too on many occasions are the fish caught, although there is nothing binding about this.

Barbel of near record size have been taken on feeder tactics, as have many fine tench, bream, roach, dace and chub, not to mention some mighty perch. Yet because its contents of groundbait relates more to the hook bait than the particles normally associated with the block-end variety, the big fish man tends to lean more heavily on the open-ended feeder (but not always, I must emphasize). The barbel angler, for example, may well use a block-end feeder to put his carpet of maggots or whatever on the bottom and then use a portion of luncheon meat or some other kind of meat on the hook; just as the bream fisher might put his groundbait in the swim by way of an open-ended feeder but use a lobworm or two as the bait. Therefore, when dealing with this subject it's best to leave our minds as open-ended as the last-mentioned feeder, otherwise our approach will be far too rigid to succeed.

To avoid failure the hook-link or tail should be varied until some sport is forthcoming, as should the size and weight of the feeder because, just like any other method, there are absolutely no rigid rules relating to such details, the one working at any given time or place being the correct one for that particular occasion. Try it a day or two later under the very same conditions, however, and the chances are it won't work at all, and so more changes to the terminal gear are called for to drum up a bit of action again, making it very much a case of 'if at first you don't succeed then try, try again'. There really is no shorter path to success than that.

Swim feeders by their very bulk are prone to getting snagged on the bottom, and just how many now carpet the floor of the more popular rivers is beyond all reckoning, I should think – a sorry situation. Perhaps the problem could be solved by the use of some slowly soluble material which takes effect only after several days of continued immersion in water; but I guess that might be getting into the realms of science fiction.

And so on to the kind of bite detection favoured by feeder anglers. Swing-tips may well have been designed for the purpose, so suitable were they for feeder tactics, but then later along came the even more sensitive quiver-tips, and would you believe target boards, against which to measure the slightest digression of those tips at the pull of a fish? As far as I'm concerned if the fish are that disinclined to pull the tip over to a noticeable level I'm not inclined to bother with them. But of course, whatever the situation facing them some anglers will not be deprived of their buzzers, and why should they be when so many great fish have been taken when using them in conjunction with feeders? That fact goes to illustrate just one more time, I believe, that where fishing's concerned nothing is at all sacred or binding.

9 The Etceteras of Legering

The etceteras to the legerman's armoury are many and varied; and while for some it's enough to have just the minimum weight and the baited hook on the end of the line, others are not in the least happy unless they've everything going cluttering it up, from swivels to curtain rings and every imaginable bit of hardware in between. Just how necessary all this paraphernalia might be is very much open to debate. I recently spotted a pike angler with at least four swivels keeping his rig together, and God only knows how many split-rings and beads, which suddenly made me realize why some use such heavy rods – they need 'em to cast out all those etceteras!

In its correct place there's nothing at all wrong with a bit of refinement – it can be a great asset in fact. Just when extras might be used, though, is up to the individual who must assess the situation confronting him. Before venturing to add any extras to your line ask yourself if you really need them, and if so then why. You may come to the conclusion that they are more of a liability than an asset.

The idea of using most of these bits and pieces is to attempt to lure the fish directly or indirectly into a false sense of security by trying to convince it that there's nothing attached to the bait. Having gone that far we're half-way to actually catching it. But (and it is a very big but) if the extra weight of those swivels, etc., combines to produce a point of resistance in themselves then it goes without saying that we'd be better off without them. So the entire issue depends on how you see the set-up at the time of fishing. Sadly, though, some anglers are so accustomed to rigging up in a certain mode that they do so as a matter of course, without considering the reason. More's the pity, too, that others, always on the lookout for pointers, see this regalia on the would-be big-fish catcher's line and are quick to ape it, be it to their own advantage or not. And so we are smitten by yet another new trend, with everyone fishing in the same style because they consider it's the fashionable thing to do. Far better to think for yourself. You will receive far more satisfaction from even mediocre catches than you ever would by simply mimicking the next person with no thought about the reasons why. Work things out for yourself and you can make an educated guess as to the whereabouts of the fish, just what the bait should be, and also the best way of getting it to the fish without frightening them away. You will also dwell more positively on when to attach that extra split-ring or swivel to the line!

Swivels come in all shapes and sizes, and while they have always been a part of the freshwater fishing scene I doubt if they've ever been more popular than now. This is due not only to the pike angler's renewed interest (which has always been there, but rather more reluctantly in modern times, I think, because of the custom to fish with unusually large swivels for pike) but also in a lesser sense to the carp angler's adoption of them as well. This has made swivels quite acceptable again in some fields of endeavour – although I'm happy to say not in all.

Link-spring swivels, barrel swivels, Cross-Lok swivels, snap swivels, three-way swivels – they all have uses at some time, be it simply to avoid line twist or friction on the line or to act as some kind of boom; the choice is yours! When it comes to booms, though, I reckon we freshwater types still have a thing or two to learn from our saltwater brethren. Take a look at what's available there and you'll doubtless wonder as I do why some of the rigs restricted to the saltwater scene can't be steamlined more effectively to fit in with your own. It's a possibility I'll be giving some thought to in the future.

Not too many commercially made booms are obtainable at the moment, which is why many anglers make up their own. From John Roberts Fishing Tackle Developments, however, have come forth some very useful anti-tangle tube-rig booms, on which are affixed clips to take the lead. A smaller yet somewhat similar version is produced for feeder fishing, and for other forms of legering there are beads. These have a hole through which the main line passes and just below that the tiniest of pin-holes to which is tied the link. Others come with a clip to take the sinker.

To describe split-rings as being perfect circles of wire that give access to the line would be a misrepresentation, because Mustad have recently brought out a whole range of oval-shaped split-rings which at first glance appear to be better equipped to take care of our needs. They are strong, come in a couple of useful sizes and hang more naturally on the line. Only time will tell if they are to replace the more familiar completely round split-ring, but they at least offer an alternative.

Rod clips can be another great asset when carp and pike fishing especially, for they keep the line from clip to bait as taut as one would like to avoid the wind or flow from playing havoc with it and, more importantly, to give a taking fish free line from the open spool of the reel directly it pulls the line out of the clip. These are snapped on to either the butt section of the rod or nearer the tip, although some anglers have been known to fish with a clip in both places to help combat a particularly difficult wind. But remember, rod clips represent yet another point of resistance. That's their very purpose in fact, and only when the fish are taking confidently will I use them, which isn't always the case even with pike. When dead-baiting, for instance, pike have a tendency to *draw* rather than snatch at a bait. I recently witnessed several takes aborted after the line had been pulled clear of the clip, and suspect that more than likely this was due to the pike objecting in the only way they knew how to the slight pressure felt, which was by dropping the bait.

Leger beads come not only in different sizes but in different colours also! Slid down on the line to sit comfortably on the knobs holding the rigs together, they are rapidly replacing the old split-shot kind of stop which can damage the line and in so doing cause it to break at the worst possible moment – just when that lunker is right over the net! To lessen the possibility of this happening I can recall one well-known angler who decided that the only way to soften lead shot so as to make it easier on the line was to warm it in a pan over a low gas ring. But *Oh là là* – all he ever finished up with was a pan awash with molten lead!

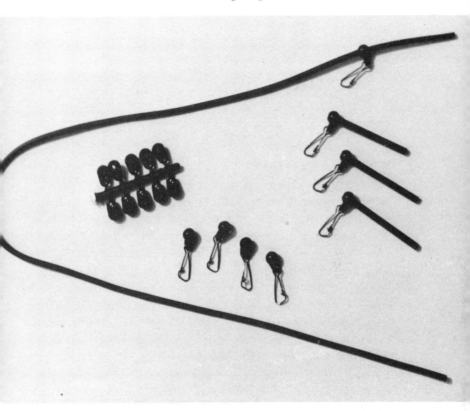

**From John Roberts have come a very useful selection of
anti-tangle booms**

10 Legering Techniques and Rigs

When it comes to legering we find more varied techniques on offer than any other branch of the sport. Each has its own role to play in the scheme of things, be it the most cherished of methods to some or the most despised of all to others; each and every one has a niche to fill at some time or other. Yet with the freedom we have to choose the one we prefer at any given time, we do tend to use each for a variety of different reasons – whether wisely or not – the main one being that whichever rig it is, it just happens to be the one the angler feels most at home with, most familiar with, or possibly it's the only one he has come into contact with.

If this is the case it is a great pity because, in effect, he is missing out on so many lost opportunities. The fostering of any one of those following could have a most pleasing and lasting effect on his future sport. For it's simply not good angling to be handicapped by entertaining only one method of catching fish – or even just a few, for that matter – and I would go so far as to say that in fact it's downright suicidal. If we all had this blinkered vision of how to go about the business then few of the many fine fish reported in the angling press each week would see the inside of a landing net in the first place.

Flexibility, then, is the password to success – or even the short-cut, if you prefer – because without it there can be no learning, and when that's gone what's left? My own interest in the sport would have withered and died long ago but for the learning process, and I dare say much the same can be said of most thinking anglers, for to ring the changes in respect not just of rigs, but of everything else connected with this pursuit of ours, goes a long way in fermenting the very ingredient which keeps us on our toes: the excitement, with our legs shaking at times in the most delightful manner as we battle with some unseen leviathan of the deep. It gives our enthusiasm more thrust, and this can come only from being inquisitive about the entire scope of angling, not just what fits in conveniently at the time; everything else tends to fall nicely into place after that.

The very idea of persevering in the same old manner year in and year out must, though, inevitably take its toll of any keenness the angler concerned had to begin with, and from there it's a pitifully short road to complete and utter rejection of angling altogether. But how does someone come to reach such a level of frustration? The answer to that question I can't begin to guess at. And yet it happens. There are also those among us who continue to fish as they always have, without a further thought as to why and with no notion of changing. But that is their prerogative, just as it is ours to ferret out more and more knowledge about fishing, and try to put it to good use; and who's to say in any case that the others aren't smitten by the innocence of their approach and enjoying it all the more for that?

But be that as it may, it seems such a sin for them to be missing out on the extra pleasure that succeeding with something different could bring them. As I've said, it's from that direction that much of my own pleasure is derived, without which angling would be lacking for me, and as much as I do have my own particular likes and dislikes pertaining to all aspects of the sport, I rarely if every turn a blind eye to a possibility that might help fill my net simply because I don't much fancy it.

Feeder tactics are a case in point. I'm not too enamoured with having those damned gadgets cluttering up my line – my approach, I hope, being a mite more subtle than that; yet I'd be a fool to condemn them out of sight just because I don't happen to like them, while knowing perfectly well that they can reap a better harvest from the water for me. Barbel fishermen swear by the feeder these days, and who am I to criticize them when, if they took the trouble to look, they'd find swim feeders in my bag too? Sure, I would rather they stayed there, but not at the cost of having a dry landing net at the end of the day.

Whenever I can, though, I'm far happier fishing running

water with nothing but a single swan-shot pinched directly to the line about six inches or so above the hook. This, on rivers and streams, represents to me the Utopia of my calling! It's also one of the finest and fastest ways of getting together a good catch of chub, and occasionally the odd barbel. And don't tell me you'd have difficulty in keeping your bait on the bottom with it in a rapid flow; I use it in the weirs, where it's not supposed to sit skulking on the bottom. It's meant to be moving down with the flow, picking up a fish here and there as it goes. And what's more, should conditions be especially kind, I'll dispense altogether with even that tiny weight, and freeline instead, because I find there's nothing quite like it for sheer exhilaration – or exasperation, should you hook into something beyond the power of your gear. For this is fairly light stuff compared with most legering trends, in which a line of three or at most four pounds test is used in conjunction with a rod and reel that will sit comfortably in your hand. We're in touch-legering territory now – the best there is – and when the opportunity to use it presents itself I'll reckon with none other.

The running leger

There really is no other way to describe a running leger other than to say it's a sinker running on the line and stopped from sliding down to the hook by a stop of some sort. It is still the rig most often adopted. It's also a very ancient technique compared with most, and probably one of the first to be developed with a bit of thought behind it; not a lot initially, I'll grant you, but enough for it to work well and win widespread acclaim none the less.

It has since been up-dated, of course, what with the incorporation of swivels etc. to add some finesse to the rig. New-style sinkers were brought into use to enhance the sensitivity of the running leger, and there's not a species of coarse fish which isn't being sought by this method for much of the time.

I'm especially fond of it because I knew of no other when a lad, and therefore graduated from it to more complex rigs; but such was my innocence about the niceties of angling that I'd

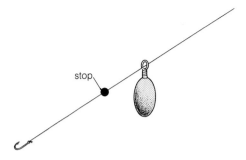

Figure 15   Straight or running leger

break the end off a matchstick and use that as a leger stop instead of a split-shot – which served its purpose well, I thought. And when later my 'bream' period arrived I really wouldn't consider any other means of taking them but on the running leger. I still revert to it whenever the need arises, although I must confess to disowning some of the leads that went with it during those early days.

Coffin leads have well outlived their usefulness by now and are rarely seen, although for holding the bottom on the running leger there's probably still none better. Indeed, there was a time when the eel-fisher especially would accommodate no other weight in his bag. He wished his bait to lie doggo on the bottom, without moving an inch if he could help it, and the flat shape of the coffin helped him to achieve this end like no other lead could. Since then, though, things have changed, and even eel fishing has been brought into the twentieth century; and why not, when there are still so many unsolved mysteries surrounding old *Anguilla anguilla*? It could be said in fact that the eel is the species we know the least about, but I feel sure we're getting there, one hesitant step at a time.

The main objection to the running leger was highlighted shortly after World War II at about the time when there was a slight stirring in angling's dormant mind. Thought was brought to bear on the adverse effect a bit of friction might have on the fish; was it possible, someone must have wondered, for them to feel the drag on the line as it passed through the hole running the length of the sinker, and so drop the bait?

Ball or bullet leads with a twist of wire added for the line to run through became the craze for a time, since they were an improvement on the hitherto popular coffin. Yet overall, leger leads haven't changed much over the years. It's their adaptation which has changed, and which in turn changed the sport of legering from what some believed to be a very slow business indeed into the fascinating challenge it affords us today. For not only are there now so many different ways of presenting the legered bait, but also combinations of each; individual interpretations of each; personal variations, adaptations, and alterations so drastic in design that often it's difficult to define where the well established ended and revolution began (sometimes for the better and occasionally for the worse). But that must be the way of it – searching for that definitive rig.

The paternoster

It's difficult to understand why, but paternostering has never been as readily accepted as most other bottom-fishing techniques, even though it's been around for as long as most and has a lot going for it when a bait needs to be fished on the bottom, just off of it, or even at mid-water. This lack of interest was, I used to think, due to the appearance of the paternoster rig, which is not in the least attractive as it hurtles in ungainly fashion through the air; yet when viewed alongside some of the carp rigs now in use I feel sure that something else must account for its disfavour. But whatever that might be there is no denying that paternostering is generally overlooked as a means of taking good fish.

That doesn't mean to say, though, that the paternoster hasn't had its moment of recognition, because it has. The fifties and sixties gave it a boost when perch were especially popular and the paternoster (a running one more so than a fixed one) was the rig promoted to catch them. It has since made tremendous headway in the pike angler's armoury, with a float or poly ball attached at times, and must by now be one of the most popular methods of taking the species by those capable of moulding the rig to their own individual needs. But overall, the paternoster –

Paternostering for perch can be most decisive, particularly when a small fish is the bait

both fixed and running – is still crying out for a bit of attention from those concerned with other kinds of fish. And that's a pity when the more tricks we have up our sleeves the more likely we are to fool the quarry.

Paternostering was the method used as soon as I was able to think for myself; and if I did happen to catch only perch and pope (ruffe) on it, so what? That's all I was after at the time. Hampton Court on the lower Thames was the venue, and worm invariably the bait. God only knows why, but we kids weren't at all into maggots then, perhaps it was the sixpence (2½p) demanded for a tinful that put us off! By then, though, I was reading all that I could lay my hands on about fishing – which wasn't a lot at the time, just about enough to make me think in terms of the terminal gear I was using, and that paternostering called for a pear-shaped lead. Well, I'm now inclined to believe

that any sinker would have served its purpose just as well then, and within reason would probably do so now, since ideally a paternoster should be fished on a tight line with the rod tip kept at a sharp angle to the surface of the water to ensure that it is kept tight, and the bait anchored at the desired distance from the bottom or top, depending on your ploy. However, thinking anglers, I'm bound to repeat again, are apt to make the rig work for their own special requirements and so adapt it accordingly.

Basically (and it's the basic set-up that I'm concerned with here) the paternoster has a fixed lead at the bottom of the cast, be that direct to the reel line or on a separate length of line, and the hook – most definitely on a separate piece of line – is attached by one means or another at a given distance above the weight. Exactly what that distance should be can only be decided upon at the water's edge, but as a rough guide I would suggest eighteen inches as a starting point, and more or perhaps even less should circumstances demand it. To be more specific than that without knowing all the relevant details is an impossibility!

Minute split-rings and swivels are mainly used for the purpose of attaching the hook-link, which effectively need be no longer than twelve or eighteen inches, but again I cannot be too specific because there are variations to suit certain needs. The only point I am prepared to be adamant about is the use of one hook only. Others, I know, swear by a two-hook arrangement, and nobody can question their success. Yet the likelihood of one hook becoming caught up in snags while a fish is fighting for its freedom on the other presents a risk I'd rather not take.

A running paternoster is identical to a fixed one other than that the hook-link runs freely through the same split-ring or swivel, to which at the other end is affixed the lead. The metal link of whatever kind is then stopped from sliding down to the bait, of course, by the usual split-shot, plastic stopper or bead.

As great as this rig is for pike or perch fishing, in its fixed

---

A fine 20-pound pike taken from the moat at Leeds Castle in Kent on paternostered deadbait

---

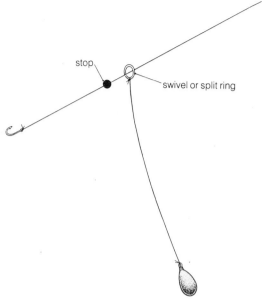

Figure 16   Running paternoster

form it was chosen often enough in the past for bream too, and
what gigantic catches it made, the likes of which we're never
likely to see again! And it's even been adapted to penetrate the
carp scene. So like most methods it comes and goes, with
changes here and there to bring it in line with whatever trends
are in vogue at the time. But to think of the paternoster as first
and foremost a way to keep a bait lurking near the bottom is a
sensible approach. Any alterations should be made with that in
mind.

The link-leger

The link-leger, generally attributed to Peter Stone, reached the
peak of its popularity in the late fifties and early sixties, a
position from which it hasn't slipped one iota. The link-leger is,
as its name implies, a leger lead fished on a separate link from
the hook and, when one thinks about it, it is the complete
opposite to the paternoster rig, which carries the hook above the
weight rather than below it. Quite revolutionary was this idea,

since it offered all manner of possibilities so far as the lead was concerned, for anything from a single swan-shot to the largest of weights could be used just as effectively. Perhaps more importantly, in a situation where the angler found himself roving from swim to swim, as for example when chubbing on river or stream, the lead could be changed in a flash to meet even the most daunting flow without the chore of having to reassemble the entire terminal gear as was necessary with the old running leger technique. And that to my mind is why the link-leger became such a firm favourite in a very short space of time for all kinds of fish.

But let's not forget its main advantage, the one it was evolved for; and that's to do with sensitivity. For instead of having the line run directly through the hole in the lead – as in the running leger fashion of old – we now have it passing through a swivel or tiny split-ring. This results in a lot less friction for a fish to detect as it takes the bait. Apart from this, it's also worth considering the distance a lead can be kept from the bait once on the bottom, since that is bound to have some bearing on spooking the fish. With the lead at an angle, rather than practically on top of the bait as in the case of the running leger, it does I believe give us just a little bit more edge over the quarry.

A short length of line (usually about four to six inches) has affixed to one end the weight and to the other either the swivel

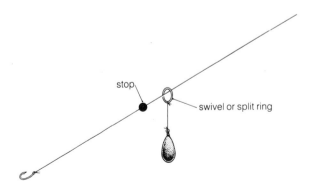

Figure 17   Link-leger

or split-ring through which the main line runs to the hook. While the swivel works just as well, if not better, it was at first the split-rings, however hard to come by, which were patronized the most. I personally went through a great deal of strife while trying to obtain a supply, and recall writing in sheer desperation to Peter Stone for some advice on the matter; back by return of post came a sample of the rings he used, and my God, they were tiny! I eventually ran a supply to ground, and still use them at times to this very day.

The whole business is kept in place by the usual stop (I'm rather gone on the plastic stops now!) and all the angler need do to change the weight of the lead is to snip off the first and tie on another in its place. The drill is as simple as that, and if you're as fussy about such things as I am, then you will fully appreciate the time and trouble saved while at the water's edge. For me at least that's a particularly big saving, for not only am I likely to try different weights in the same swim but different baits as well. It's a fact of life that the baits themselves often dictate the size of the sinker to be used as much as the flow, and the flow may well have a different effect altogether on the terminal end of the gear when the bait's changed. That's a point to be kept firmly in mind if you hope to achieve the best a water can possibly offer.

The link-leger is applicable equally to running water and still water, and fish of all kinds are consistently taken on it. In some cases, though, you might not recognize it for what it is since no other arrangement so far as the business end of the gear is concerned has undergone more alteration from what was at one time accepted as a perfectly normal rig.

I must emphasize again that in terms of rigs at least, we must move forever forward, to wherever experimentation may lead us, for only then can we learn to decipher more of the fish's ways: its characteristics and habits, and all else that goes into making it one of nature's most complex creations.

To return to the link-leger, I lean most heavily towards the tried and trusted swan-shot link, mainly because it represents the kind of simple approach I like, but also because it offers such a vast range in the amount of substitute lead I can fish with. A

A fighting fish is drawn near to the net after falling foul of an Arlesey bomb weighted link-leger

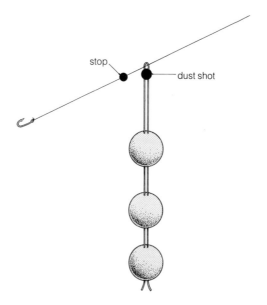

Figure 18   Swan shot link-leger

shorter link of a mere few inches is looped over the reel line at the required distance from the hook, and the two ends of the loop pinched together by a small split-shot to hold it in place. The swan-shot forming the actual leger weight are added, and the weight can be changed in a trice by adding or removing shot.

This, then, is the rig I use most often when fishing fairly fast water, and usually that means for barbel or chub, although in practice there's scarcely a species of fish I haven't taken on it at some time or other, so adaptable is it. But for still water I prefer to stick to the original idea of the link-leger, if I'm not actually freelining, that is, which I'll do whenever I believe streamlining better suits that particular situation.

The rolling leger

Particularly suited to swiftly flowing water is the rolling-leger technique. The existence of this technique is due in the first instance to the adaptation by Dick Walker of the familiar pear-shaped leger lead into the extremely versatile Arlesey bomb, which because of its torpedo shape can be rolled along the bottom at the angler's whim, taking the bait along with it. In this way, then, the greatest volume of water can be searched in the shortest possible time – a substantial asset in itself to any form of fishing. Even more pertinent, many species – quite apart from the barbel and chub for which these tactics were originally intended – prefer to take a bait that's drifting down with the stream rather than a more stationary one, which is why long-trotting with a float continues to be such an outstanding success.

To roll a leger one simply selects a sinker that is just heavy enough to hold bottom against the flow on its own without sitting there obstinately like a jackal and refusing to budge. Too heavy and it'll move clumsily if at all; too light and it will take off on its own downstream without ever touching bottom, and without ever giving a single fish in the vicinity a chance to sample its wares. Therefore it is imperative to have the size of the sinker just right.

Arlesey bombs, because of their shape and attached swivel, are ideal for the job, although with experience you can manage well enough with any suitably rounded leger lead. These work just as effectively as an Arlesey bomb when run on the line like a straight leger, providing of course that their weight is just right for the prevailing conditions. Without the swivel we're bumping rather than rolling the bait – but who's to take notice of that? Not the fish that's for sure, because their attention will be focused on other things, like the big lively worm on the hook that is trickling down with the stream. So the bait is on the move, which is the object of the whole exercise!

A cast upstream is made to begin with, to a point where it can still be controlled, and with the line tightened the tip of the rod is then lifted to coax the bait upon its way. The line is kept taut at all times, not just to keep the bait on the move but also to detect when it's taken. And there's no better means of getting to grips with this desirable end to one's efforts than feeling for the fish to take. Bites when they come will be fast and furious, believe me, for with the bait forever on the move, should a fish with designs on it hesitate in the least then the currents will whisk it away.

The touch-legering technique

It's necessary then to hold the rod in the hand throughout each cast when rolling or bumping a bait through the swim, and to feel for them with the line snaked around a finger in the touch-legering way. There are no other really worthwhile alternatives for detecting bites in these circumstances, which for some is the main attraction. Through the line they are in sensitive touch with the bait: poised and ready to strike at the least provocation. It does pay when applying these tactics, though, to dip the tip of the rod occasionally so as to rest the bait briefly on the bottom, where it will waver enticingly in the flow. Then, after thirty seconds or so (unless taken of course), lift the tip to set the bait in motion again, searching every nook and cranny of the river bed.

Bearing in mind that the sight of the bait rather than its smell is what will attract the fish, I lean towards larger baits on the hook; imagine, if you can, the odds of a single maggot being spotted and taken in the flow. Not a lot of hope there, I shouldn't think, which is why I prefer to offer as bait something that can be seen quite clearly as it makes its way downstream, such as a big fat lobworm, for instance, or perhaps even two. In fact, up to a point anything will serve that will not go unnoticed as it travels to journey's end – until intercepted by a fish more

Rolling a leger in the race of a weirpool

inquisitive than most, that is, for there's little doubt that some fish take a moving bait merely because it is moving, and not because they happened to be hungry at the time. Therefore, if it's big and bulky, and a fish might just eat it, why not give it a try? The results can be quite startling.

The proof of the pudding is in the eating, so they say. And so is the catching of fish! I've tackled the most rapid rivers in this country, and not a few overseas, yet still have to see the day when a bait lying motionless on the bottom of this type of water outfished one that was permitted to trickle down with the flow. Indeed, on the Hampshire Avon at Christchurch, rolling a leger was at one time the most popular approach of all for those wishing to fish without a float, and great catches of barbel and chub were made there. Suffice it to say then that this water, like the nearby River Stour, lent itself beautifully to the roving-bait technique, and huge numbers of anglers gleefully got into the act.

Deeper water, such as that found in parts of the Thames, is

A lower Thames weirpool which lends itself perfectly to the rolling leger technique

---

not so easily fished in this manner, although experienced anglers still do well enough there. Results can never compare favourably with those of the Avon or Stour but that's due to fish stocks rather than tactics, and in the more rapid regions of the Thames a rolling leger is well worth giving a whirl.

Upstream legering

There occasionally comes a time when for one reason or another circumstances are such that the only way to present a bait on the bottom is by legering it against, or upstream of, the flow. Obstacles such as trees or bushes preventing an easy cast are the most obvious, while in effect any number of different reasons can exist to make casting the bait upstream instead of downstream a wiser choice. Some anglers simply prefer to leger upstream because under certain conditions it affords them the very best chance of succeeding.

Take for instance the classic example of a river or stream filled with streamer weed. Beneath that weed most of the fish will be hiding, and in the angler's mind waiting most patiently for a bait to reach them. Normally getting the bait to the fish is attempted either by casting downstream in front of the weed in the hope that a fish will venture from it in order to investigate the bait, or by dragging the bait back through the weed after casting so as to bring it nearer to where the bulk of the fish are. Both approaches will bring forth the required result some of the time, but it must also be stressed that each has its drawbacks. With the first method we're relying on the fish to leave the security of its hidey-hole in the weed to get at the bait, and with the second easing the bait back through the weed can cause the fish to be spooked and put them off the very idea of feeding for quite a considerable time.

Therefore, what we have left is upstream legering, which allows us to put the bait above the fish and let the natural path of the currents carry it along the bottom and right into the very heart of the weed growth, if we so desire, with far less disturbance than dragging it back against the flow. This is how many worthwhile barbel and chub are taken from rivers noted for their streamer weed, such as the Avon, the Kennet and the Stour, and it's all down to logical thought and application.

As always, and more especially in this case, the weight of the sinker must be just right to counter-balance the flow to the degree where it will be persuaded to go along with the flow easily yet gradually, without causing too much of a rumpus as it slowly penetrates the weed, if that's how you intend to tempt the fish therein; if not, then a smaller weight than usual can still be used when upstream legering to hold the bait stationary on the bottom. It should be light enough for a mere tightening up of the line to dislodge it, unless any prevailing wind calls for a very tight line, when it will pay to use a heavier lead to hold bottom more purposefully.

A longer than normal tail (hook-link) might also be advisable to carry the bait just a little further from its anchorage and deeper into the domain of the fish sought, although if hook-ups become a problem then a shortening of the tail might become necessary. It's a matter of learning by trial and error as you go along. Most baits can be worked in this fashion on a rolling leger but if the flow is such as to allow a freelined bait to be used then this would be my first choice.

For bite detection I like to tighten up to the lead slightly and feel for the fish by the touch-legering method. Watching the tip can be equally effective, but bear in mind that a slackening of the line instead of a good hearty tug might now be the signal as a fish takes. Instead of stealing line through the sinker to create a pull, a fish is more likely to release whatever pressure may still be evident and give you a slack line bite. Any unnatural movement of the line could well be a take, and should be acted upon accordingly. So if watching the tip for bites, keep it at a sharp angle to the bait, and anticipate the tip springing up, rather than being pulled down when the bait is snatched.

At this delightful stage of the game a good sweep back of the rod will be necessary to take up the slack and drive the hook home firmly. It is also beneficial to be ambidextrous with your casting skills, for two hands which are equally adept at punching out a bait are decidedly better than one! But with or without that splendid quirk of nature, upstream legering is definitely the way to fish when its downstream counterpart seems less than inclined to bring in the fish. Indeed, I've known some anglers to specialize in these tactics to very good effect, and nobody questions their motives because results, like actions, speak louder than words!

The leadless leger

Freelining – or leadless line fishing as it used to be called – has undoubtedly been with us for a very long time; perhaps from the earliest awakening of mankind. Since it represents the simplest ever method of fishing with a rod and line, freeline angling must have taken place long before even a stone or some other kind of weight was attached to the line (vine?) in order to get a bait out to the fish or down to where they lay on the bottom before being swept away. That's the way I see it, anyhow. However, to bring the matter within the sphere of our interest

A good tench taken on a leadless line

today, Dick Walker is again the man credited with the modern method's conception. Throughout the centuries, fishermen must have been using the leadless line to good effect but Dick Walker was the man who gave us freeline fishing by rediscovering and promoting it. Without him most of us would never have heard of it, let alone tried it, which would have been a pity, because in my opinion, leadless line fishing is the ultimate in terms of still-water fishing when conditions are just right for it.

Sadly, it's out of fashion now, and therefore rarely used. I adopt the method for tench, particularly during the opening weeks, and find that it scores over a more orthodox leger remarkably well. Depth is a deciding factor in respect of when to use it. I prefer water of ten feet or less which cuts down on the angle of the rod-tip to the bait, since to take full advantage of the lack of drag now evident, the entire set-up from reel to bait should ideally run in a straight line to minimize the last remaining hint of friction. Disposing of friction altogether is the aim but with the water presenting its own barrier to the line, and therefore also to a taking fish, it seems that whatever we do to try to overcome it, drag there will always be to some degree. All we can do is lessen it as best we can.

Rods, then, are positioned in rests to form the desirable straight line to the bait, and usually the bail-arm of the reel is left open so no resistance is experienced there. And finally, with everything now set up a fish can make off with the bait in complete confidence, and without the least hint of suspicion that something's attached to it.

Here then is the reason why a leadless line works so remarkably well: there's nothing to clutter up the line or scare off the fish. But as far as I'm concerned there's a good deal more to it than that. Imagine, for instance, nothing between you and the fish during the course of battle other than the hook and the line. It's a different ball game altogether then, I can tell you, because without the weight of the lead to deaden proceedings the fight is a lot more hectic, more widespread, and decidedly more breathtaking. Add to that the fact that such a rig makes less disturbance when entering the water and there's another advantage to be had from freeline fishing. Overall it is the most gratifying method of taking fish.

Obviously, to cast a bait without the aid of a sinker is no small task unless one has the right gear for the game. It's the rod that now has to do the job of the lead and punch that bait out to where we need it. But most legering rods not built like broomsticks will tackle the task admirably. Light line helps, and with a bit of stiffness in the rod's tip, quite reasonable distances should be attainable and without too much effort by those striving for a bit more finesse in their approach. But don't try putting a couple of maggots out. Remember, the weight of the bait is all there is, so think about its size and weight.

Dick Walker used balls of paste the size of duck's eggs, which worked fine for him. A mothball size is my usual offering, which works just as well for me, taking into account the line I use for the purpose, which will be of either four or six pounds test. A heavier line would obviously call for a correspondingly heavy bait to bring forth the same required result – a point often missed when venturing to cast a bait without a lead for the first time. But it does get easier with practice, that much I promise, because like most things worth pursuing it's just a matter of persevering with something which, on reflection, is simplicity itself.

Indeed, I'm often casting out just a single lobworm into a weirpool for chub as well as into a dormant farm pond; but for anything lighter than that a fly rod with an elongated butt will serve better, and when used in conjunction with the smallest of reels will open up to the angler all kinds of new possibilities in so far as fishing baits on the bottom are concerned. Yes, he could even return to his maggots, although with so many more natural baits now on offer I'd expect him to be a bit more imaginative than that.

Soluble sinkers

In an attempt to increase the restricted distances attainable with a leadless line, various soluble means were tried over the years, of which few were anywhere near acceptable for the level required. These included the more obvious chunks of salt and sugar cubes, both of which did work up to a point since the aim was to add some weight to the terminal end of the gear for the sole purpose of casting it farther than even a fairly large bait would allow on its own. Even soluble tablets such as Alka-Seltzer were brought into play, attached close to the baited hook by means of a separate length of line to which a weight of some kind was fixed.

A particular mint with a hole in the middle lent itself even more ideally to the task because attaching it via that hole simplified the entire operation of arranging the rig. It did, however, take rather a long time to disappear altogether, and in searching for something that might dissolve more quickly than a mint I stumbled upon the idea of using ice-cubes instead. Ice is nothing but frozen water, of course, and we all know what a heavy substance water is: absolutely perfect for the job at hand, or so I reckoned, but unless you have previously tried to transport ice cubes any distance, which I hadn't, you give little thought to the possibility of them melting. So all I finished up with at the waterside on my very first attempt at using ice cubes was a can of cold water instead! On my next trip I carried the ice cubes in a thermos flask! 'Great!' I exclaimed while affixing the first of my revolutionary sinkers to the line by way of a wire hook – I'd had the foresight to add these to the cubes before freezing. And it was with great aplomb that I made the first cast, launching the very idea of soluble-sinker fishing right into the twenty-first century! I was a mite put out by the absence of a suitable audience to witness this historical feat, but as it turned out it was just as well no-one was there. I hadn't even entertained the idea that ice might be more buoyant than I had previously supposed. I realized it when I spotted my sinker bobbing on the surface way out. I was livid! Yet at least half of my plan had worked for the bait really was well out, albeit well off the bottom as well.

What was lacking in my experimental sinkers was the weight to take them down to the fish on the bottom. After that need was assessed it took no great effort to come up with the idea of adding this all-important ingredient to the sinkers while still at the liquid stage. I used gravel, which proved to be admirable for the purpose.

But I did not need to experiment further to produce sinkers of a like nature after that, because really there was no need. A form of dissolving tape came on to the market just after my breakthrough with ice cubes. Almost anything could be tied to it to serve as the weight, including the odd assortment of nuts and bolts which we all have stock-piled somewhere at home in readiness for the job that never materializes. So in the end, my perseverance with soluble sinkers could be said to have been a waste of time. But as in all angling, experimentation to meet even the most daunting challenge is half the fun.

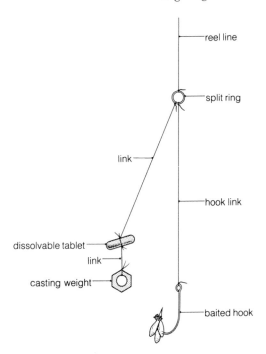

reel line

split ring

link

hook link

dissolvable tablet

link

casting weight

baited hook

Figure 19   Soluble sinker

The bolt-rig system

My first gut reaction to the bolt-rig was one of extreme distaste, and dissatisfaction with the fact that we had reached such a level as to expect the fish we seek actually to do what can often be deemed the hard part by hooking themselves. I then recalled a little gadget that had drifted over from the United States just after the last war, which was described simply as a 'self-inserting hook'. As far as I remember, a minute spring was fitted to this devil's creation in one way or another which the fish activated as soon as it mouthed the bait, and so became hooked.

Now perhaps it was sheer sporting pride that caused that little bit of nonsense to be laughed out of the few tackle dealers' shops that dared to entertain it and right back across the water to the other side of the Atlantic, where I hope it perished in hell. But what happened in the meantime, I asked myself, to allow a rig which is the same in principle as that infernal Yankee hook to raise its evil head again after all these years?

With time we have learnt that more good than bad comes from our looking back and reclaiming from the past that which should never have been left there in the first place, and to many that includes the bolt-rig, which has indeed been around for a lot longer that most of us would suppose. Largely, however, those fishing in a manner to encourage the fish to hook themselves were probably quite unaware of the fact as they went about it and might attempt to deny such an allegation now. But I assure you that the evidence is there to prove the case; it cannot be refuted.

In action, any rig that is fished tight up to the reel becomes in effect a bolt-rig, in that it permits a taking fish to come smack-up against enough resistance to panic it into searing off and in so doing affixing itself quite accidentally to the hook. How many times, I wonder, in whatever the circumstances, have anglers quite unwittingly used the bolt-rig policy in order to catch fish? I have for years been an advocate of watching the rod-top for bites (and still am), and so have practised a form of bolt-rig fishing. It would seem that most of us who leger have been guilty of doing just that for years. A few dozen years must have elapsed since I fished from a concrete apron jutting out over a deep riverside channel where pleasure craft came to tie up, and from where many nice bags of perch were taken on worms which were presented on a heavy sinker straight down from the tip of the rod. Indeed, no other way appeared to produce the goods just then, other than the technique of casting out and retrieving until the lead, and more pointedly the bait, was just off the bed of the water at our feet. With that much done it was then a matter of waiting a mere minute or two for the rod-tip to bow in answer to yet another fish at the bait. The bolt-rig effect in action? You can bet on it! And never a single take can I recall missing!

God only knows how many barbel I've taken in just this fashion, because I detect them at the bait either by 'feeling' for them with the rod held in the hand or by watching the rod-tip for takes; both of which call for me to be in direct touch with the lead and the bait, and which must over the years have resulted in an awful lot of fish hooking themselves. I have always suspected that this could be the case, and said as much in print almost twenty-five years ago, much to the chagrin of one well-known angling scribe, I might add, who in turn set about systematically dissecting me in print because of his contention that barbel rarely if ever hooked themselves.

Fortunately, as was his way, Dick Walker came to the rescue a week or two later by saying in his column in *Angling Times* that barbel did indeed hook themselves, on far more occasions than we could possibly credit them for; so I knew for sure then that I was definitely progressing along the right lines with my barbel fishing. So much so in fact that I was the first to suggest the formation of the original Barbel Catchers' Club, of which Dick himself became a member, albeit somewhat reluctantly – which goes some way in explaining perhaps why Dick was a bit remiss in getting the rotary newsletter off to the other ten or so members on time (where are those letters now, I wonder, and would dearly love to know?).

Barbel, then, are very prone to hooking themselves on the kind of set-up described here, and perhaps also to a lesser degree when an angler is stret-pegging with a float, because there still exists that tautness from bait to reel or rod-tip; and much the same can be said of almost any method which incorporates this self-hooking facility. This we have to live with, but to go out of one's way to achieve as much deliberately is, I feel, quite another matter altogether, and one which carries the heading of luck as opposed to skill a bit too blatantly for my liking – but each to his own I suppose.

Since the purpose of this book is to describe and to discuss in detail the various legering tactics and trends as well as to pass judgement on each, bolt-rig fishing cannot be omitted. The focal point in bolt-rig angling is the lead itself. This is unnaturally heavy, all things being equal, and has little relationship to either the distance needed to cast a bait to the fish or the prevailing rate of the water's flow. Both of these are normally highly relevant considerations to be taken into account when choosing a leger lead, whereas in this instance alone a lead larger than would be necessary at other times is used to make the fish bolt when encountering the resistance it obviously creates – hence the term 'bolt' – and it is by this action of bolting away in alarm from such a disagreeable drag that sets the hook well and truly into the jaws of the unsuspecting fish.

Usually a fixed lead is used for this purpose, but due to those using it being taken to task of late over fish breaking free and having to tow heavy weights around with them until their dying days (which wasn't expected to be far off, with the ever-present risk of the line becoming entangled with some rubbish on the bottom from which the fish could never escape), emphasis is now being placed more fully on foul-proof rigs. This is particularly true of carp anglers, who tend to be more associated with this rig, and from whom the most positive moves have come to dispel all chance of a fish being left to die in such an awful manner.

In its most crude format a bolt-rig consists of an unusually heavy sinker on the line which is kept in place by a stop of some sort above and below it, so that the lead doesn't move an inch. Thankfully, however, this very basic bolt-rig is now shunned by most, and I sincerely hope that once it arrives there it will stay firmly in the past, for we've no need of it whatsoever.

The hair-rig

In complete contrast to the negative qualities of the bolt-rig is the hair-rig. Although not a complete technique in itself the hair-rig, pioneered some years back by Lenny Middleton and Kevin Maddocks for carp fishing, does nevertheless have the amazing capacity to change even the most mundane rig into something quite spectacular. Normally terminal gear comes to an end at the hook, but the presence of the hair carries it just a little bit further – be it just an inch or so – to divorce the hook from the bait.

Now without the weight of a hook to influence its actions the bait will behave in a more natural manner – but that's just one aspect of the advantages to be gained from fishing the hair. Another is that since the fish takes the bait on the hair, and in so doing also sucks in the bare hook secured to a stronger link,

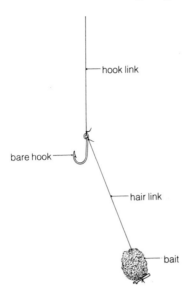

Figure 20   Hair-rig

the hair as such has no strain to absorb and so can be fashioned from the most gossamer of line. Ironically, it is in the weakness that the true strength of the hair is to be found, because no longer are we plagued by the doubtful business of trying to tempt big fish on line that is correspondingly heavy and coarse in relation to their size. Nor, indeed, do we have to reduce the weight of line to solicit bites to the extent that often it's simply too flimsy to bring the fish in, and they are sadly left hooked and trailing broken lines.

A tale I once heard on the Throop Fishery section of the Dorset Stour will better serve to illustrate this matter. It concerns God only knows how many barbel which were allowed to escape the net because the angler was so adamant about getting at least some bites from them. It took place during the last phase of a period when barbel could be spotted with ease but were rarely coaxed into taking a bait, so painfully shy of the business end of the angler's gear were they – until, that is, the angler in question decided that at all costs he would at least hook into some of them, and unfortunately he did.

The outcome of this was very drastic as far as the barbel were concerned because he actually found them on the feed, and was soon being busted left, right and centre on the cotton-like excuse for a line he was bent on using to get the better of their finicky ways. And yet remarkably, he at last managed to persuade one right to the net, and eventually another until, at the end of the day, it was his proud boast that he had actually taken no fewer than eight fine barbel. Just how many he left behind him with hooks still protruding from their mouths is anybody's guess. He had in his own eyes succeeded where so many had failed, and the carnage left in his wake was obviously of no consequence to him.

It is just as well then that with the coming of the hair a situation like that should not repeat itself, although it does remain doubtful if buffoons like the one above would have the mental faculty even to begin to appreciate the great advantages that the hair-rig offers. Not only would he have hooked many of those barbel on it, he would also have brought a sight more to the net, simply by attaching to the hair a line more capable of subduing them.

Easy enough to use once you've got the measure of it, tying on a hair can at first be a quite fiddly affair, especially if the hands are numb with the cold. Tie on one end of the hair and the other will resist all your efforts to make it good and secure, by which time the first end will have come adrift and need to be tied all over again. Such was the frustration that I first came up against, that from then on I decided out of sheer desperation to make up my hairs at home beforehand instead. What I did was to tie a tiny rubber floatcap to one end of the hair, which slipped nicely over the point of the hook, and then to the other end attached one of the mini boilies I intended to use for bait. The target fish were very late-in-the-season tench, it being the month of October by then, and I was well pleased to discover that my own little contribution really worked a treat.

Needless to say, though, special needles for baiting up with

A fine pair of tench taken on the hair-rig

boilies are now available, as well as equally special beads to hold the boily more securely in place, not to mention hooks designed with a spike on which to fish it. I am rather keen on what is known as the Bill Quinlan Bristle Rig which, as its name implies, is simply a bristle made from plastic or pinched from a broom that is tied to the business end of the hair. One end is sharpened to pierce the boily with ease, which is then pulled back against the bristle to hold it firmly in place. It's as well to remember, though, that baits other than boilies can be fished on a hair, and in the case of the Quinlan rig it is suggested that the bristle be tied in the middle and passed right through softer baits.

Tied at the very beginning more frequently to the bend of the hook, the trend now is to affix the hair to the eye of the hook instead to gain the maximum penetrating power of the latter. But because it's popular with the carp fisher, I expect that more improved methods of presenting a bait on the hair are just a tick or two of the clock away.

11   The False Serenity of Summer

However delightful to the appreciative eye, or indeed, however soothing to tangled nerves at the end of a long week spent at work-bench or desk, to dangle a bait into the water on a warm midsummer's afternoon is definitely not on my list of favourite pastimes – not if I seriously want to catch fish it isn't. Because as nice as it is to sit back devouring the sweet scents of summer, the drifting drone of a nearby bumble-bee or the sight of a beautiful butterfly alighting at the tip of my rod on gossamer wings, such conditions can hardly be conducive to good results.

Both water and air temperatures will be high now, and the serenity of the stream trickling past will lose much of its enchantment if moving just a little too placidly for my liking, and possibly more so for the finned inhabitants therein. They'll doubtless be distressed by these seemingly idyllic conditions, if not altogether desperate for a jolly good dose of life-giving oxygen. And if seriously lacking in depth or flow, that lovely low summer stream can very quickly turn into a stream of death instead for the fish.

How fortunate for them and us, then, that small oxygen-aerated pockets of relief for the fish are normally to be found somewhere – and it doesn't take a brain like Einstein's to deduce that here's where most of the fish will be gathered at times such as these: anywhere which has that extra bit of flow, or, failing that, where the water is deep enough in a sheltered bank-side swim still to contain a fair amount of oxygen and offer at the same time some protection from that daunting sun.

Cabbage patches and other oxygen-giving growths in the water must also inevitably attract fish, and he who finds them is in with some chance of a decent catch if conversant enough with the leger. This style of fishing is more imaginative than most,

and flexible to the point where one could almost say (although there are bound to be exceptions to prove me wrong) that when all else fails the bait legered with some thought behind it will usually find a way. And at this time of year there will be many anglers trying; for what place is more attractive than a glistening summer stream?

The main thrust of whatever flow is left will be in the middle of the stream where there may be some movement, be it little more than a meandering mist-shrouded dribble. If it's the best on offer to the fish searching as they will be by now for some respite from discomfort, then that's where they'll be. They will also take whatever relief a bend in the river carrying some extra flow will afford them. But if there's one to be had then the angler is better advised at this time of year to turn to a weir-race instead. The weirs, more so now than ever before, will be supportive of all kinds of fish, seeking some relief from the torrid heat of the day. Such is their discomfort at times, however, that their feeding can scarcely be expected to be anything like normal. That's why they ought to be approached with some delicacy now, using as fine a line and tail as is reasonably possible, which is put on the water just as delicately, with barely a ripple if it's at all feasible. The fish will be edgy, more cautious than usual, and less inclined to feed with any urgency. What we offer must be gently worked down to them. They are not likely to be interested in a whopping great mouthful on the hook – neither would we be when suffering under the influence of such heat. Therefore I would suggest something for bait that is small but tantalizing: a maggot or two perhaps, or a small red worm, which when presented lightly might just work. In fact, careful feeder tactics could score here by releasing a trail of maggots to tempt the fish out of their stupor, or failing that a single swan-shotted line with a similar bait on the end, provided it's fished with feeling. Don't let impulsiveness take over and ruin the entire object of this gentle approach.

Stream of death? It could be in summer!

When there's little oxygen in the main river concentrate instead on the weirs, for that's where the fish will be

I must say I don't feel comfortable about disturbing the fish on these occasions when they have enough problems to cope with, so should such circumstances arise, then I'm more likely than ever to turn to the still waters instead. They are generally deeper than the rivers and tend to fare better, despite their lack of flow – although even here the fish have been known to become distressed at the height of a heatwave, especially in the shallower lakes and pits. The legendary giant carp of Redmire, for instance, began to suffer during the long hot summer of 1976, and considerable concern about their welfare was felt by members of the syndicate controlling the water at the time. A pump and an oxygen meter were kept in readiness to monitor the levels of dissolving oxygen and to put more in when the need arose. It was due to such diligent care and observation of the water that the carp in Redmire Pool survived the onslaught of that extended dry season, for which we can be extremely grateful. For whether you've been fortunate enough to fish Redmire or not (and I haven't), this water does in a sense belong to us all as a part of our heritage.

126

12 Autumn: Season of Optimism

Autumn is the period when, if we're lucky weather-wise, we may enjoy many of the attributes of the glorious summer fishing scene combined with a few of those that winter has in store. It's about now that the pike fisher traditionally begins to make his move. The old idea of pike fishing being a lost cause until the first frost could be seen on the ground was exploded as a myth long ago, yet still the great majority wait, and that is no bad thing, I reckon, for what we have here is not just a run-of-the-mill fishing trip but a planned endeavour to get amongst old *Esox lucius*, and for the truly dedicated no other time will do.

Methods won't have changed much, but with the pike a little less erratic now it might pay on the rivers, as well as the lakes and pits, to linger just a while longer in any one place. Much will depend on the water, of course, and how the angler personally reads the situation facing him. A bait lying dead on the bottom might succeed now when it failed during warmer conditions, but I'd have to opt for something a bit more imaginative than that and bring in a paternoster perhaps, which is just weighty enough to hold bottom against the more pronounced flow of a river in autumn without resisting a flick of the rod top to move it on a bit.

The barbel catchers will be more purposefully abroad, at this time, knowing that not only will their favourite quarry be feeding in earnest now that temperatures have dropped to an acceptable level and the river has begun to move more to the fishes' liking, but also that they will test the skill of those hoping to encounter them at the end of a line in a manner it would be hard pushed to aspire to earlier in the year. The streamer weed in which the barbel shelter during the warmer months will begin to wither now, making the search for them with a rolling leger

Light-legering the autumn stream

just a mite more profitable than a month or two back. And with them as usual will be the chub – in far better condition now, and zeroed in on more substantial fare than was previously available to help maintain and build that condition right up until the time arrives to propagate the species later on in the new year.

The tench will still be inclined to feed, but just as the winter scene embraces the pike with more feeling, so do those still and silently breezeless summer dawns epitomize in their rising tendrils of early morning mist the picture we have in mind of what tench fishing means. But make no mistake about it, the tench will still be there and feeding, but more on sweetcorn or boilies than bread or maggots, and if you haven't hooked a tench well into the season then you can't possibly appreciate just how much better they fight then. Also, if you cursed the delicate approach necessary to take them consistently at high summer, then be prepared to scale down on line strengths and hooks even more as the summer wears on to autumn proper, for they really do need prompting to take a bait now, even on a hair-rig, so keep sinkers extremely light and your entire gear free of resistance, and you should be in a position to take a fair sprinkling of tench right throughout the year.

With still a fair portion of fry about, perch will continue to frequent their usual lairs, although unlike that other predator the pike, I find the perch more on the move now, and a more interesting proposition by far than they were during the opening months of the season. I look forward to taking them in and around the weirs as well as the quieter reaches of a river further downstream, and rather more out of the currents unless they are still relatively slack in movement. Be the bait a dead or a live fish I'll try a swan-shot or two pinched about twelve inches or so from the hook first so as not to restrict the live bait and hopefully get the water to instil into the dead bait enough wavering in the flow to suggest to the fish that it might just have enough of a flicker of life left in it to warrant their further investigation.

And now let's consider the roach, the better specimens of which are often taken on the leger, even though most are sought with the float. This idea may upset a few anglers who know their business as well as anyone, and who will say in all sincerity that their catches of roach with a float cannot be compared with what others wind in on the leger. I agree, for these anglers are a unique breed, having mastered the intricacies of long-trotting a lifetime ago, and they have the waters on tap on which their particular style of roaching can be practised with little hindrance compared with that which they would meet on the Thames, for example – even there, my approach with a fantastically light leger would probably offer no contest to their expertise with a float. But I'm more concerned about the less skilful with a float, fishing a water that lends itself to the undeniably more difficult task of long-trotting a bait below a float far less than some of the country's more illustrious waters.

But do what you can with a leger on the Thames and the like and you may well be surprised at what you reel in. Now we're not discussing three-pounders here, but fish of half that weight, worthy fish none the less for the water from whence they came. What I especially like fooling them on are thumbnail-sized pieces of cheese on as fine a leger as I can get away with in a frisky flow. And that might be met anywhere, from the apron of a weir to the galloping mid-stream flow of a straight stretch of water, assuming it's still relatively clean. Perhaps a normal running leger with a whisper of weight to get the bait down to the fish would be my first choice of presenting the bait. If not, then a swan-shot or two crimped directly to the line or on a link would probably serve just as well, as might a kernel or two of corn on the hook, or even a pinch of bread; but cheese, I find, most certainly sorts out the better roach.

The carp will still be at home, with an invitation to catch them if you can, for it was proved beyond any reasonable doubt long ago that they weren't just a species of the summer season and are now taken, albeit not frequently, during the coldest months of winter too, by those prepared to explore such an avenue. During the months of autumn they are still at the forefront of the carp angler's thoughts – as are the bream of their followers. So all things being equal, we are viewing the overall picture of coarse fishing at the zenith of potentiality. If left with only one period in which I could fish, my choice would have to be throughout the autumn every time.

Fishing the late autumn River Thames

13 Legering with the Winter Wand

Fishing in winter is not so gleefully adhered to as in the earlier months, of course, what with the inclement weather the angler is forced to endure. It can be bad enough to put the uninitiated off the sport for life. Yet if the angler can only find the driving power to complete the course he soon discovers that whatever disadvantages he has to put up with, having a dry landing net is not among them, for legering at this time of year can be the most hectic period of all. Roach, perch, dace, pike, barbel and chub – they're all on offer now, and will be inclined to feed more ravenously so as to build up their strength for the trials and tribulations of the breeding season that lies ahead.

It must have been approaching that time when I not only saw but actually caught my first barbel; not that it broke any records but my own, and yet in the eyes of a fishing-mad fourteen-year-old no barbel had ever been bigger than the three-pounder I captured on that pleasant wintry day. And would you believe that almost immediately after this memorable catch a chub of about the same size followed it into the net? My friends and I were ecstatic. Kids in those days just didn't catch rod-benders, at least not without the supervision of an adult, and for us these two beauties represented the turning point. There was to be no going back to gudgeon and the like after that – it was more barbel, and more chub, fished for purposely now that we knew it could be done, and even after all these years I still much prefer to seek them when summer has been long gone.

I think they're a lot easier to pinpoint in winter, with the passage of the flow more definable, and therefore simpler to read. Wherever the signs tell me to fish close in because that's where anything edible will be carried by the stream to the fish, then fish close in I will. That's a lot easier than trying to combat

Legering in the slacks in winter on the River Thames

a wicked midstream flow, in which there probably won't be much in the way of food or fish, the former having been swept into the edge and the latter having finned their way speedily after it.

Big and bulky baits are what I like to use now, because they can be seen better in heavily coloured water, an added attraction that will not be missed by the fish. A normal running leger should also prove its worth. A bit of stability to make the bait toe the line so to speak mightn't be such a bad thing when the flow is really strong, even right in the edge under the banks. Unless the angler is fortunate enough to find a depression in the bank or similar feature to create a slack or eddy of sorts, he'll have little choice but to fish downstream to a distance he can still control. As often happens in circumstances like this, he shouldn't be in the least surprised either if his bait finishes up just a few feet from the bank. But that's okay; he should just leave it there if some pretence of a depth is present, for left undisturbed as they usually are with fewer anglers about, fish of all kinds will venture closer into the edge than one would suspect, and even more so when forced to take up temporary residence there because of the pummelling flow. It stands to reason then that that's where your bait ought to be, and it's a mistake made by many to try to beat the force of that flow by using a dirty great sinker to hold a bait out in the middle of it. Why even try, when the fish are actually so much more within reach?

Find the right place and approach it sensibly and anything from a barbel to a bream might be yours, for often during these conditions it's very much a case of Hobson's choice. Roach, too, will be present, and will take with as much relish as a chub whatever the bait, within reason, even if it does seem to be more of a mouthful than a roach could possibly handle. I've had good roach take lobworms and even five grains of corn on too many occasions to think of it as anything unusual, and the same goes for a good dollop of chub-sized cheese! In fact, I took my first ever pike on a lump of cheese. I suspect it went into a spin on the end of my line and fooled the pike into thinking it was chasing something more to its liking – but I wasn't complaining.

Pike also hole up close to the bank in winter, which does as usual make a lot of sense when you realize that here is where their tucker is. It's only by thinking about these things rationally that we come to learn a good deal more about the quarry. 'Try to think like a fish' is an expression I've heard enough times over the years. So try saying to yourself, 'now where would I be if I were a fish?' – and you'll be surprised at just how often you get the answer right!

But of course, reading the water is essential. Without that only mediocre results can be expected. It's not a subject to be easily taught, either, for experience is the best tutor. But what an absorbing lesson it can turn out to be, what with trying to note each minute little detail below the surface as well as upon it. It's one facet of angling I'll never grow tired of. And the messages carried by the water are there for all to see, should they take the trouble to look in the first place and to interpret them with some understanding of a species.

Without hesitation I must say that the most inspiring bit of detective work I've done like this (for that's what it is after all) concerned the capture of a trout on a worm. It wasn't a particularly big trout (about three pounds) but exceptional for the stream, which was flooded and nigh on unfishable at the time, with the water over its banks. Yet simply by standing there and observing the entire action of the water I was left in no doubt whatsoever where the fish were sheltering from the push of the flow; it was an area of about the size of a dining-room table, and not more than twelve inches deep. Nevertheless I gave it a try, and couldn't have been more surprised than the fish itself when it took the worm that must have dropped right on its nose! It was the only one I got, but having the thought put into your fishing rewarded in that manner makes the prize not only special but memorable too.

The back end of the season is the time for big fish. But watch that flow. If it's too heavy they'll be tucked away close into the edge

14 Legering in the Dark

I seem to have spent my entire life fishing and the better part of it has been devoted to night fishing. I had no say about that at the beginning but was simply dragged along year after year, too young to protest, even assuming I had had a mind to; but there never was any question of that. I simply adored being out there on those dark and eerie banks all night, and from my very early teens I'd night-fish alone if necessary, so engulfed was I in the sport. And now, after all those long years, I'm as keen as I ever was.

Rain, snow, hailstones and storms – I've sat through them all in my time. One of the most unforgettable occasions was when some friends and I were set on taking some low-in-the-winter bream. Low in the winter? Now that's an understatement if ever there was one! Right in the grip of winter would better describe the weather; for just how often I wonder does the temperature drop to such a degree as to freeze not only the line to the rod rings (which we tend to accept as half-way normal for this time of year) but the inside of a hard-boiled egg also (which isn't in the least normal in my experience). It was frozen solid, and as much as I love fishing at night I doubt if I'd survive another excursion like that. But we did catch our bream.

Other nights have, of course, been much more pleasant as I've fished in shirt sleeves right through until the unwelcome dawn, so enjoyable have the hours of darkness been, and so busy at times as the action reached a level that it scarcely ever can during the day. Even predatory fish can go on a feeding spree at night, with the exception of perch. I've only taken the occasional perch at night in this country but there's a particular stream in Australia where night or day I couldn't put a bait in the water for trout without the perch devouring it in a trice. I did beat

**The best bream fishing is invariably to be had at night.
Author poses with an 8-pounder**

them in the end, though, by using large slimy slugs, which the
trout enjoyed but the perch wanted nothing to do with.

So where does the great appeal of fishing at night lie? I guess
the answer to that question is different for different people. One
of the most obvious is that the fish, relatively undisturbed at that
time, become less cautious and are therefore more inclined to
go about their business naturally, unhurriedly, now that the

sense of danger permeating the hours of daylight has subsided. It will be reduced on heavily fished waters, and perhaps be gone altogether on those where day, and particularly night, fishing is followed only spasmodically. And that, of course, gives us a better chance particularly with the bigger fish which concern me the most.

I feel free at this time to approach the task before me in my own way, without the need to conform to what others do, how they fish, or what they use for bait. For there are times during the day when you can be constrained or coerced by others. I was recently fishing a picturesque stretch of the tiny River Colne in the south from where a few double-figure barbel had fought their way to the net (not mine, I'm sorry to say). I arrived before dawn at this hot-spot to secure a swim and be ready with a bait out for when the barbel chose to feed. I wanted to tempt them on worms, so I put a few free offerings out and followed this up with a couple of good-sized lobs on a number four hook, then settled back to await developments. But no sooner did I feel totally happy with all aspects of my approach than along came another angler and down went his kit with a mighty thud next to my own. He then proceeded to lay the obligatory carpet of hemp in what was, by virtue of me being there first, my swim. Well, live and let live, I say, but not at the cost of a day's fishing, and since this 'poacher' had now effectively ruined my chances completely of catching on worms without the added stimulant of the pile of particle feed he'd put in, I left to try, without success, elsewhere. In terms of fashionable barbel fishing his was the right approach; but I dislike following trends blindly, even if they do produce the goods at times. I prefer to do things my way and night fishing allows me more often than not to do just that. And that's one of the big advantages it offers me.

Also by being out on the water before dusk, right throughout

A session on the 'night shift' shows – on the face of the author as well as in the size of the tench, which went a healthy 7 lbs

---

the night and at dawn as well, I and others of a like nature are far more likely to be there with baits out when the fish need them most. But of course, that's only the tip of the iceberg. What night fishing conjures up for me personally is a lot more than that. The greatest joy of all comes from just being there, alone with my thoughts.

The noises are different at night; sounds with a softness that can only be detected in the dark, more noticeable without the harsh clamour of daylight to compete with. But there are moments when I can't resist looking behind me when fishing a weir at night. The darkness around me is total but never completely silent. Always at the weirpool there is something a little disturbing, be it just the rush of the water or the unaccountable things that go bump in the night.

If you've never tried night fishing then now's as good a time as any to give it a go, and I promise you'll never regret it. What I think is required most of the angler bound for his very first fishing venture after dark is confidence in himself and in the fact that he is now on the water at the best possible time for catching something special. That, and a firm resolve to stay and see the rising of the morning mist now that he has committed himself to as much, is all that is required of him. Everything else will fall naturally into place as the angler becomes more accustomed to fishing in the dark, and it's not so terribly difficult, believe me.

First there's nothing to be gained from being cold, wet and miserable out there on the bank, and a good deal to be lost, such as your full concentration on the matter at hand if your main priority turns out to be one of desperately trying to keep warm and dry. So whatever the cost in cartage, do yourself a favour: go to any length to keep warm and dry, otherwise, if you're unfortunate enough to pick a particularly bad night for your debut, you may never go night fishing again. Drink plenty of warm liquids. One of the best I've found for really hitting the spot on a colder than normal night is an Oxo cube, which is quick and easy to make. Before all else, though, make sure you're at the waterside long before dark, not only to familiarize yourself with your surroundings before night falls but also to make absolutely certain that everything is at the ready and within reach while there's still enough light to attend to such things. With the rods set in their supports and fishing, the landing net should also be made up and ready at the water's edge, and the keepnet, if you must use one, pegged out in a position in the water where it won't be troublesome throughout the night.

With bite buzzers all the rage now there might not be any call for a light, but I happen to be old-fashioned and romantic enough to appreciate just how much even a weak and feeble little light at night can help transform the bleakest scene into a warm, comforting one instead. Your bobbins hang at the point of focus, poised and ready to take on a life of their own in the subdued illumination from your tiny light. Don't be put off by other people; providing that whatever kind of illumination you use is for you and nobody else there can be no reason for others to object to it.

A good, reasonably powerful torch is also necessary for netting fish – a task hair-raising enough in the light of day when a big fish is drawn near the net. Only recently I lost a very good tench at the rim of the net simply because the torch I fumbled with in the dark was inadequate for my needs; so do take care not to be caught out on that one. For more general use I prefer one of the flexible type of torches which can be clipped to a jacket, leaving my hands free for tying hooks and the like. Always at hand, they're a boon to some and a great comfort to others who are unused to fishing at night. I can't agree with the suggestion that the night fisher operate completely without lights. What on earth is to be gained by fiddling about in the dark like that? Nothing at all that I'm aware of, and even to try seems a bit ridiculous.

The illumination that I'm talking about has no adverse effect on the fish and I think it's a fallacy to insist otherwise, although others will vehemently disagree with me. I have in the past deliberately gone fish-spotting with a powerful flashlight at night, and while I can't say with any certainty that the beam intruding on the fish in slumber wasn't noticed, I can quite categorically state that it didn't disturb them in the least. I'm obviously not recommending this as a general practice – what I did with the light was most stealthily done. But it was also a good test, so do not be discouraged when it comes to the sensible use of lights at night, the word *sensible* being the operative one.

I used hurricane lamps at the very beginning of my nocturnal stints, which years later were replaced by pressure lamps, or Tilly lamps as they were commonly known, but these days when I opt for some illumination (and that's only ever on still water) I invariably use a nightlight in a tiny jar. It gives just enough light to serve its purpose without souring relations with those fishing close by. Others may choose to use a buzzer or betalight, or possibly a twist of tin-foil trailing away from the reel, which they might just hear rustling across the grass when a fish takes. I'll also often wrap a sliver of silver foil around the tip when watching for bites on a river or stream at night. It actually reflects all the light available out there in open country under the stars. But I'm less than happy about using it as a butt indicator, because when it gets damp it tends to stick to the line and get jammed in the rings, as I've learned to my sorrow; so I'm extra careful whenever using this means of detecting takes.

Be wary also when using two or more rods at night, or you're sure to have a hooked fish on one entangling itself in the other, especially if it just happens to be an eel on the end. I do not in the least envy you the problems you'll have then, having had enough of a similar nature of my own in the past. At such times not even a searchlight will help you out of that predicament!

15 Using Multiple Rods

How many rods should an angler use? That's a debate that raises its troublesome head quite frequently, for water officials and fishery managements have long had rulings in force about this, which naturally vary from one authority to the next. This has caused some resentment to those who feel justified in complaining that while they are restricted to the use of only two rods in their locality, the more fortunate elsewhere can quite legally get away with fishing with four.

Inevitably there are circumstances in which four or even more rods per angler could be handled quite adequately, while in others a single rod is all that anyone could cope with. If there must be laws about such things they should be founded on angling tactics and the species concerned.

I was amused at one time to witness the folly of an angler who got bogged down with more rods than he could possibly manage when I was chasing trout on a Victorian (Australian) stream. He was entangled in a barbed-wire fence when I came upon him, and it soon became apparent that he was going nowhere at all without my help, laden down as he was with rods and affixed by his pants to the fence. God only knows how he'd managed earlier, because he was quite obviously returning to his car when I met him and had therefore struggled with this same disagreeable barrier on his way to the river. I offered to lend him a hand, held his rods up high as he did his Harry Houdini act, and asked if he'd had any luck.

'Not a damned touch, mate,' came the expected reply. 'And I've tried everything – worms on the bottom, flies on the top, and still they didn't want to know. I even put the old spinner in each swim before trying them with baits or a fly, but nothing at all seemed to move them.'

Weighed down as he was with his assortment of gear, the poor fellow had left nothing to chance as he'd muddled through the day with his fly, spinning and bottom fishing outfits, yet had caught nothing at all. But this didn't surprise me. I've seen too many anglers put a spinner through the water before lobbing a bait out, and how on earth they can expect a fish to stick around unconcernedly waiting for a bait to appear on the bottom while the water about its head is flogged to death by a heavy lure, I've no idea.

Presumably, however, not even this joker would have attempted to fish all the styles he was concerned with at the same time, which is a point to be considered when discussing the use of multiple rods. That they have their worth at times cannot be denied, and I'm unfortunate in that the waters I have permits to fish all stipulate the use of two rods only. That's fine for most of the time, but there are periods when a third or perhaps even a fourth rod wouldn't go amiss: when the tench are playing their silly game of catch-me-if-you-can, for instance, for when in that mood there's practically no chance at all of catching them, simply because they flatly refuse to feed. It is at such times that I would like to experiment a little with something completely different from the norm on the hook, without removing the more regular bait from one of the rods in case the tench should just happen to come on the feed again. An extra rod or two in action then could make a difference to the outcome of the session.

Carp fishing emphasizes the need for multiple baits in the water, if only to have all corners covered and lessen the long wait often experienced for a positive take. And much the same can be said of pike fishing! But a note of caution must be in order here: just how many rods can an angler master with a show of efficiency combined with a sense of responsibility to the

More than a single rod to concentrate on would put the match angler into a spin! Here the net is being dried out having been well filled by one rod

fish sought? We're already being bombarded with the campaign to take better care of pike when hooked, and at the top of the list of priorities as far as that movement is concerned is the drive to strike quickly so as to avoid deep-hooking the fish. So can the means to this end be accomplished by having a row of rods all fishing at the same time? I think not. The chance is forever present when piking or having two runs to deal with simultaneously, so how about three or four? Don't say it could never happen, because it could – and what then of the fish lying doggo on the bottom swallowing the bait and the hooks without interference because the angler is too busy battling with another at the time? Makes you think about the wisdom of using a battery of rods. It might not on occasion be such a good idea after all.

When it comes to river fishing I can think of only three instances when I would normally use at best two rods, never mind a handful, and that's when fishing for pike, perch or eels, each one of which can be frustratingly slow in providing some sport for much of the time, and to have an extra bait out for the likes of those species makes a good deal of sense to me. Other than that I'm very much a one-rod man when tackling flowing water, for barbel or chub will inevitably be the aim, and I will not jeopardize my chances of getting amongst them by attempting to manage more than a single rod. It would be impossible anyway, with the touch-legering style I usually adopt.

But on the still-water scene I can see no reason whatsoever why an angler shouldn't use as many as he can profitably handle. The decision should be his and his alone, as must the responsibility that goes hand in hand with however many rods he brings into play. Without that sense of responsibility he shouldn't be fishing in the first place.

16 Bites that Vary

The very technicalities of legering ensure that there will, to some degree, be diverse options as to how particular species of fish take a bait and, more to the point, exactly how that is depicted on the bite detector, rod tip or line, all of which are at some time used for the purpose by the discerning angler.

In the old days the methods used were so gross that anything short of a mighty tug wouldn't have registered. Resistance was not a factor to be reckoned with then. The chub, for instance, were not above dragging the entire outfit along the bank, so keen were they to get at the bait; and when thinking in terms of the barge-pole-like rods used then, with those great heavy Nottingham reels attached, you will perhaps appreciate the combined weight that the chub moved off with quite happily, until stopped in their tracks. But how many did we miss, if any, because we'd no idea they were at the bait? Now that's a question which has haunted me for a long time.

Trying to rid my gear of all resistance to a taking fish has been a hobby-horse of mine for years. I've written about it extensively, because I'm a firm believer in presenting a bait as naturally and as delicately to the fish as I can possibly manage, and go to great pains to ensure that everything else concerned falls in line with that. Yet the experience we have is entirely founded on the past, and we must continue to look back and learn. So perhaps we should consider the possibility that we might on occasion operate with too much of a sensitive touch; that the ultra-sensitive and complex rigs and bite detectors used nowadays may be too progressive in their functioning, causing the fish to react to them in a way which their natural instincts don't allow for, but which does bring about the twitches, false runs and every other unacceptable indication that something is

Chub swim on a Wessex river, where good takes can often be depended upon

at the bait. 'Line bites', for instance, is a term thrown around with all the agility of a ready-made excuse for failing to connect with a taking fish. It is a description of a line movement that wasn't around in my day, even when we did possess tackle capable of registering as much. A bite was then a bite – miss it and that was down to the angler, not down to the fish blowing kisses at the line; it's a temptation today to dismiss every bite missed as nothing more positive than a line bite!

But to move on to tremors, twitches, or even line-bites if they are your forte, in rivers and streams the depth and flow of the currents bear heavily on how a fish will intercept and take a bait. My theory is that in a fast and deep swim, such as will be found in some weirpools, or in a river forced to flow rapidly by flood, the fish have little time to examine an offering in minute detail before the currents snatch it away. They are therefore reduced to grabbing what they can and being thankful for it, all of which is there to be seen in the bite. I realized more years back than I care to remember that, with exceptions of course, I had come to expect more positive takes when tackling such conditions. The slacker, shallower reaches of a river produced, generally, fewer of these suicidal attempts to get at the bait. In complete contrast to the demonic flow of the deep water, think instead of a maundering swim with comparatively little depth; why should the fish make a beeline for a morsel fluttering down to the bottom with the same kind of drive as those residing in the fast, deep water swims, when there's little or no risk at all of the currents whisking it away? The only reason I can see is the presence of more fish with designs on the food.

Everything else related to how a fish bites should logically rest with how the bait is presented and the means to detect when it is taken, and to a lesser degree what that bait might be.

17 Three Ways with the Leger

Many long and fairly fruitful years with a fishing rod in my hand have passed since I first began to appreciate the full potential of having more than one legering technique at my disposal, and the species responsible for my awakening was tench. I had until then been daunted by the fact that the tench had hitherto kept their distance from me. But after years of trying I finally caught one, about three inches long, when attempting to snatch a few silver bream on the float at first light. And that one tiny tench did the trick, for I became hooked on the species and when, a few years later, the opportunity to fish for better tench came, I didn't hesitate. I was determined to tackle them with renewed strength and vigour. I was older, more capable of approaching them in a systematic manner.

I had also decided to search for them with the leger, and since three vastly different waters were on offer each had to be assessed in turn regarding the tactics most likely to succeed. There was nothing fancy, hair-rigs and the like being unheard of in those days. My confrontation with each water would, I knew, represent a challenge of the highest thought-provoking order to one still relatively uninitiated in the ways of tench and their seductively still environment. If you can imagine a small natural lake surrounded by reeds and bulrushes, and containing more than enough tench for the few anglers who fished for them, then you will have some idea of the water that first captured my attention. In depth it varied from a maximum of about twenty feet in the middle to around three feet in the margins, and while it was generally fished with a sliding float, I persevered with a weightless leger and was soon into the fish.

The takes were quite spectacular, line being stripped from the open spool of the reel, and I recall wondering at the time if these were peculiar to the fish here or whether the lack of resistance they felt when taking the bait was responsible for these delightful runs. I correctly guessed that the latter was the cause because, when fishing at the other end of the lake with a couple of swan-shot on the line, bites were nowhere near as dramatic, and I came to appreciate in time the benefits to be had with an unweighted bait, and still turn to one whenever the chance occurs.

The next water I visited was nothing like the first, and was in actual fact a large gravel pit of unknown depth. It also had the reputation of holding some huge tench (by the accepted standard of those days), but hard as I tried I was not to get amongst them. The water was far too deep for normal leadless-line work, and the bottom appeared to be covered in soft, black mud. There was evidence enough of this to be seen on the weighted terminal end of the gear, which succeeded only in burying itself in the mud. But the link-leger was making its presence felt by then and by using one I got the better of that unsavoury bottom to a degree and managed to tempt enough middling-sized tench to make my effort worth while.

It was the third and final water, however, that really got the adrenalin flowing, for it was little more than a pond, but an attractive one nevertheless, with an air of mystery you could cut with a knife. It was choked with weed and, so I'd heard, good tench. It had an overall depth of about six feet, which I considered to be just right for a freeline approach, but I hadn't taken into account the thick weed, of course. For there was the line lying across it with the bait still visible at mid-water, and had legering not had such a tenacious hold on me I would have done the sensible thing and float-fished instead, since there were clear patches in the weed in which I could have managed a float-fished bait quite easily.

But no, it had to be the leger, and I won in the end by using a fixed lead on the line that took the bait through the weed and down to the fish on the bottom. Again they were of no great size – just big enough to put a delightful curve into my brand new MK IV Avon rod, which shows how long ago it was – but to have succeeded in a situation in which failure was so much more likely

After years of struggling to catch even one, the author finally found the path to better tench – but still can't help admiring each and every one!

gave me enormous satisfaction. It also goes to show that in comparison with the legering enthusiast, the fly, float or spinning fanatic can do little to overcome whatever the difficulties encountered other than to change his pattern, style or design. When it comes to legering an entirely new concept can be brought into play on the spot, so versatile are the techniques involved.

18 The Carp Angler's Contribution

Of course, it was Dick Walker and his cronies who first started the ball rolling, way back, because more than anything else he made us think both about the fish we sought and how we ought to go about seeking them. From there on in it was all systems go! And I personally can scarcely think of a single thing concerned with legering that Dick didn't somehow influence. I must have made it perfectly clear by now that I was and still am a staunch Dick Walker disciple. The fact is that without Dick and his like we would hardly have progressed an inch, for those following were influenced enough by the Walker era to carry its innovative thinking forward, which is how the situation stands today.

So don't be too hard on the dedicated carp anglers; instead, pinch whatever they come up with and use it to suit your own ends, for if there's a particular problem prevailing that's concerned with the still-water scene especially, then you can bet your life that sooner or later it will be the carp anglers who solve it, for they seem to be more adept at applying themselves to the task of isolating such difficulties so that they can be dealt with more efficiently.

Among the carp angler's contributions to the sport as a whole must be included the first sensible rod support and the electric bite buzzer, both of which have long been used in all areas of legering. The boily, too, was originally of course created as a carp bait – but how the tench relish them! It must be said, however, that some concern has been voiced in the past as to the adverse effect on the fish's health these boilies and certain kinds of nuts now in use as bait might have. That they packed on weight in an extraordinary fashion in some waters cannot be denied. 'Grotesque – like huge fat cows,' was one description given of high-protein-fed carp, which were too bloated to fight well on the end of the line. It's been a while, though, since I last heard a derogatory remark like that, so perhaps the position wasn't so desperate after all.

One thing that does continue to puzzle me about the use of boilies nevertheless is why, if they are supposedly only brought in when other, more regular baits have failed because of fishing pressure, as is claimed, boilies by the thousand are immediately dumped into unknown waters as a matter of course – as was so obviously the case when the famed carp of Lake Cassein in the south of France began to beckon to carp anglers on this side of the Channel. Over they went and in went the boilies, into a water which was considered at the time to be far from over-fished. Makes you question the credibility of some of these moralistic mutterings, doesn't it?

But I must say that in my opinion the most innovative brainchild of all from this particular division of the sport has got to be the hair-rig. Imagine presenting a bait to the fish, not on the heavy line required to bring it in but on a fine hair-like length instead, which doesn't even have a hook attached! Now that's the devious kind of development I can really appreciate, because in a single stroke it has made the lot of not just the carp angler, but of those who use hair-rigs regularly for other species also, a more satisfying and fulfilling one. Every time I use it I marvel all over again at the sheer simplicity of thought around which it revolves.

The rigs on which the hair is attached are many and legendary; but containing the ever-changing element that carp fishing does, new and more sophisticated terminal arrangements are being born almost daily. Therefore, by the time this book goes to press any such rigs mentioned here will almost certainly be quite obsolete; so I really see no point in discussing them further, other than to say that the subject is a most complex one about which several books could, and indeed have been written which are concerned with nothing else.

19 The Final Word: Swan Deaths vs the Angler's Lead

'Thousands of swans killed by anglers' lead!' So screamed the media in bold headlines to launch an attack on us that was without equal in the long history of angling. 'Killers of God's creation', they called us, and worse. So what then was the true situation behind such condemnatory comments? Were anglers indeed responsible for the deaths of thousands of swans? That there were swans' deaths of our making cannot be denied, the evidence to support such claims being clear enough. Swans were dying with our lead inside them, although nowhere near as many as the outrageous figures quoted, and in that respect alone anglers were unfairly accused.

As is only natural under such circumstances, we looked elsewhere for a scapegoat. The shotgun enthusiasts, for example – don't they discharge more lead in a day than we would in a lifetime? I used to be one myself and feel obliged to confess that they do. In point of fact, though, the pellets from a shotgun are not as pure as anglers' lead and therefore nowhere near as toxic or harmful to wildlife in the sense being discussed here. They are harder, and therefore more likely to pass through an animal or bird if swallowed, so the experts tell me. And if we care to go way back, there was a time when our own split-shots were nothing but shotgun pellets with slits in them to take the line. It is relevant to note that when we did use those pellets for shot, the deaths of swans from them were scarcely if ever heard of. The problems arose only when split-shot was specifically manufactured to make them less brittle, which called for a higher concentration of lead.

Eventually on 1 January 1987 a total ban was announced of lead weights and shots of less than 28·35 gm (equivalent to 1 oz), with the exception of the smallest split-shot, below 0·06 gm, which is equivalent to a number 8. There did appear to be problems in the beginning, as this meant in effect that all the leads legermen used were banned. But happily we have coped very well indeed. Substitute lead was developed and, as a bonus, several new-style sinkers that I for one wouldn't want to be without. The battle to preserve the rejected lead is now over and lost – and a good thing too, to my mind.

Since the ban came into force there have been encouraging signs to suggest that the swan population of the River Thames especially is getting steadily stronger, with an increase in the Oxford area of 31 per cent and a most impressive 53 per cent on the Lower Thames; which goes to show that anglers have listened, and have learned to manage remarkably well in a situation that wasn't that difficult to deal with after all.

Index